APPLES AND ANDERSONS

An Autobiographical Account of a Child's War

Anne Hathaway

ARTHUR H. STOCKWELL LTD
Torrs Park, Ilfracombe, Devon, EX34 8BA
Established 1898
www.ahstockwell.co.uk

ISBN 978-0-7223-4995-3
Printed in Great Britain by
Arthur H. Stockwell Ltd
Torrs Park ` Ilfracombe
Devon EX34 8BA

CHAPTER 1

'Dad's not going!'

My sister Joan, twelve years old, looked up from the task of feeding the baby and scowled. She was sitting on the steps outside the French windows, the fat, dark-haired baby resting in the hammock of the skirt that hung between her legs, suddenly indignant that the feeding bottle had been tugged from her chubby lips. My mother was battling with the hairbrush, endeavouring to tease the knots and tangles out of my unruly six-year-old hair, frowning slightly as she concentrated. My father sat in his carver chair with three-year-old Susan on his knee.

'War's a terrible thing,' he said. 'I was in the last one, so I might not have to go this time.' He paused, then said, 'It won't last long – shouldn't think so anyway.'

'I don't want you to go!' Joan's voice was shrill with fear.

War. It didn't mean a thing to me. I was more concerned with the sharp snag and pull of the hairbrush. I stood, head bowed, tears pricking the backs of my eyes while it continued its relentless work. I tried to concentrate on the pattern of the lino on the floor, but it kept disappearing in the patches void of any colour where countless feet had shuffled and scuffed as we all sat round the large heavy table at breakfast, dinner, tea and supper, seven days a week, year in, year out. My eyes, blurred and blinking, moved across to the peg-rug in front of the hearth, handmade by Mum and Dad from strips of every bit of hard-wearing material they had been able to collect: John's coat, Betty's skirt, Lila's blazer, Dad's overcoat, Mum's winter dress, Joan's pinafore dress, Susan's pink leggings, Pat's pram blanket and, there, making up one corner, my grey skirt. All those pieces had been woven into an oblong of sacking to make a thick, comfortable rug.

Mum's hand came up under my chin, tapping gently but firmly for me to raise my head. Now I could see *The Gleaners* hanging on the wall opposite – pretty ladies in bonnets and pinafores, collecting ears of wheat after the harvesters had finished their work. This was one of my favourite pictures – it symbolised tranquillity in a house full of noise and bustle. There were seven of us children, all dark-haired with grey eyes. Betty was the eldest and eighteen at this time, then came Lila, Joan, John, the only boy, me, Susan and finally Pat, the baby. As always happens in families, we were all so alike but so different. Betty was 'elegant'; Lila, the efficient one; Joan, all smiles; John, always up to some prank or other; me, skinny as a stick insect and a bit of a rebel; Susan, sweet and fairylike; and Pat, noisy, demanding and pouting.

We were a large, healthy, happy family. Dad was the boss, Mum the comforter; we children were a rowdy, loving, squabbling crowd. Dad drove buses for the Oxford City Motor Company in the days when drivers were inspected before taking their buses out on the road. They had to have clean hands and nails, good neat haircuts and shiny boots and buttons because they would be in the public eye, and in those days such things were very important. He would set off on his bike long before we were stirring in the mornings to be at the depot at six o'clock, often not returning home until we younger ones were again in our nightdresses and ready for bed. He worked long shifts because of all the mouths he had to feed, bodies to clothe and feet to shoe. Overtime was as important to him as breathing.

At forty, he was a strong, muscular man with a good head of dark hair, pale-grey eyes, high cheekbones and thin lips. We all thought him a very handsome man and I know Mum did, too. After eating his evening meal, which was a good plateful of vegetables, meat and gravy, or rabbit stew, or a meat pie, followed always by a pudding, he would stand up, stretch, take his tobacco tin from the mantelpiece and roll himself a cigarette, the end of which, usually bereft of any shreds of tobacco, would flare and settle to a steady burn.

'Off to bed, you lot,' he'd say. 'And no nonsense up there.'

Then he'd disappear into his shed in the garden to repair our shoes, mend a puncture or put the wheel back on the pushchair. There was always something that needed attention. We would lie in our beds with the blankets over our heads so we could talk without being heard and listen to the tap-tap of his snob's hammer. He was very particular about our shoes and said that a person's character could be told by the shine on their shoes. His work in the shed completed, he would roll another cigarette and stroll to the top of the garden, where we kept the chickens. There were always a dozen or so hens in residence along with a feisty cockerel to ensure Christmas dinner and a constant supply of fresh eggs. He knew that during the day Mum had done her bit towards their welfare by preparing and feeding, watering and collecting, so all he had to do was drop the flap that covered the little doorway to their run and secure it with a hook and hasp. Finally he would fill the coal bucket for the following day and stack a few logs under the verandah by the back door so they were handy for Mum next day. By this time, we younger ones would be fast asleep and Betty, being the eldest, would be tiptoeing between the beds as she prepared for bed.

Mum's days were so full that I can hardly remember her sitting down and just relaxing. She was last to sit down at the table at mealtimes and the first to get up. She was up with Dad in the mornings to cut his sandwiches and fill his bottle with tea (Thermos flasks were a luxury). She would cook him a breakfast and stand at the window to wave him off before going back into the kitchen to set the table for ours, laying out the bowls and spoons for our porridge. Dad had laid the fire the previous night before going to bed, so she only had to put a match to it if the day proved to be chilly. Then we would hear through the drowsy mists of waking, 'Breakfast's all but ready' and 'Betty, you'll miss your bus' and 'Lila, you'll be late' and, after a short while, 'Do I hear someone moving up there?'

Throughout the day she would wash and cook, iron and clean, setting the table again at midday because we all, except Dad, came home for dinner. Then, after we had all gone again, she would load

Pat and Susan into the big battleship of a pram and walk the mile or so to the shops, with every so often a visit to the baby clinic to get the bouncing baby weighed, beaming with pride when the nurse smiled and said, 'Beautiful baby, beautiful baby.' But she worried about little Susan, thin and pale, quiet and shy. 'Never mind, Mrs Hathaway,' the nurse would say. 'Your Nan is like a sparrow, but healthy as I don't know what.' I was always 'Nan'.

I think Mum liked teatime best of all. The main cooking of the day was over and done with at midday, so tea was easy with bread and jam or meat paste, cakes and a huge pot-bellied pot of tea taking centre stage. She could relax a bit after cutting the bread, and we would all sit and chat about school and work and argue a bit over the tart with the most jam in it. If the chatter got too noisy Mum would tap the teapot with a spoon, just to restore a little calm. We all knew what the tap-tap-tap meant and the chitter-chatter stopped, but only momentarily. Gradually our voices would again rise to a crescendo as we all did our best to tell the 'best' news or to argue over the last rock cake.

Seven o'clock was bedtime, summer and winter – not a minute before or a second after. Mum would now be seated in the little black armchair, her sewing box on the floor by her feet, a pile of socks on her lap – so many socks! always socks! – but sometimes she would get a change and there'd be buttons to sew on or some knicker elastic to thread. Her eyes never left her work, but she knew exactly when the clock on the mantelpiece reached seven.

Very quietly she would say, 'Seven o'clock,' and one by one we would leave our jigsaw puzzles or drawing books and trail off to wash our grubby hands and faces and comb our hair, then file past her for a goodnight kiss and make our way up the wooden hill, as she called the stairs.

There were only three bedrooms in our house – one for Mum and Dad with a cot for baby Pat, and one for Betty, Lila and Joan with a double bed for Betty and Lila and a single for Joan. They had to share a cupboard for their clothes and a dressing table, which we carefully divided into three. Betty's third held her bottle of Soir de Paris (which she treasured so much she didn't use it) and her Pond's face powder. Lila's had her neat little pile of hankies and her hairbrush and mirror. At fifteen, although she went to work, make-up was definitely not allowed. Joan's was piled up with her prized collection of *Girls' Crystal* magazines and film-star books. There was a rickety cane-seated chair under the window and a wooden shoe rack which Grampy had made for them, and by the side of each bed a small oval mat, crocheted by Grandma Ward to protect their feet from the icy-cold lino.

In the third bedroom was another double bed, which Susan and I shared, much to my horror as Susan still had the occasional disaster in the middle of the night – she wetted the bed. I would plead with Mum to separate us, but there was nowhere else to put me so I just had to put up with it. I had another reason to dislike my sleeping arrangements – John slept opposite in his little iron bed and would insist on telling 'ghostie' stories, stories about dragons and Gypsies that stole away little girls in the middle of the night – especially girls with the initial 'N'. He would speak in a weird voice so that in the darkness I found it hard to remember that it was just John and not some horrible hobgoblin waiting to pounce out of the gloom and attack me and my little sister – who was normally fast asleep anyway and heard nothing of it.

Our rooms must have been the bane of Mum's life as all three of us were avid collectors. John with his soldiers and anything crawling that could live in a shoebox, Susan with her broken, chipped or torn toys who were her 'babies' and spent a very sad time wrapped in bits of rag in various tins and boxes under the bed, and me with my books, scribble pads, crayons, pencils and paints. I could not bring myself to discard a pencil if there was the minutest scrap of lead in it; some of them were so small they were difficult to hold, but they were not going into the rubbish until I said so.

Behind the door was a row of coat hooks where our Sunday clothes hung. They were hung there to avoid creasing because we had no cupboards – there was just no room – but we did have a lovely five-drawer chest and competed ferociously for space in the two 'other' drawers. John, bigger than us – and older – usually won every argument until Mum got to hear about it; then we got a fair hearing, so he didn't get away with everything!

The other very important item in our bedrooms was, of course, the potty. After all, who would want to venture out into the back garden in the middle of the night? Mum and Dad had a pretty one, decorated with delicate flowers in pale mauves and pinks, Betty and Lila's was plain blue china, Joan's white enamel with a dark-green line round the edge, as was mine and Sue's. John's was dark-green enamel. During the day these receptacles were piled high beside the lavatory to be collected as we went to bed. Mum's last words every night were, 'Don't forget the Michaels,' though for the life of me I could never understand why they were called that – but Michaels they were, even when I was bringing up my own children. Potties, to the Hathaways, have always been 'Michaels'.

So, in our snug little orderly world, poor though it was, we were happy. How Mum and Dad must have worried when war was declared. Of course, we children had no such fears. War was just headlines on a newspaper, men with posh voices talking on the wireless and we children being told, 'Shh, Dad's listening to the news.' Anyway, I had more important things to do – like learning to ride the little Fairy cycle that we shared, going to school, wondering if I'd get my sums right. Things didn't seem all that different. We still went for walks on Sunday, went to the allotment to watch Grampy Hathaway pulling carrots, played hopscotch in the street . . . It was all the same – at first.

CHAPTER 2

'We're moving,' Joan whispered to John and me as we were getting ready for school one morning.

John looked up from tying his bootlaces. 'Moving where?' he asked.

Joan's eyes twinkled. 'To a new house.'

'Can we take the chickens?' I asked, wondering who would feed them if we weren't around.

''Course, dafty,' said Joan.

I felt better – new house, OK, but the chickens had to be fed.

So move we did. Three months after the declaration of war the city council had decided that the Hathaways were a bit overcrowded and had offered us a five-bedroomed house on a new development. I can remember the hustle and bustle, but only vaguely. The most important thing to me was the fact that I had to walk! We were given bikes, carts and trolleys to push, laden with bundles, boxes and sacks, tied down with ropes and string. Lila was in charge and strode along pushing Pat in her big black pram, almost hidden under coats, blankets and cushions. The houses were so new that the paths hadn't even been made up properly and we jerked and jolted along looking for 'ours', which was number 8. That wasn't difficult because we all recognised Mr Jacobs' big red-and-brown removal van and Mr Jacobs himself, unloading our familiar bits and pieces on to the road.

'That must be it,' said Lila, and we all agreed.

I remember watching our furniture being swallowed up by that big red-brick empty house and feeling quite afraid that things were not going to continue as they had. The warmth and comfort of our old house seemed gone – gone and forgotten a little bit more with each box, chair, cup and bowl that was carried inside. The windows of the other houses in the road stared blindly at me – cold, blank stares that made me want to run and find Mum, but she was inside the empty house and I was too afraid to go inside. So I tried not to look and concentrated on Mr Jacobs and his helper, who were piling John's skeletal bed frame with rolled blankets and pillows. The pillows kept rolling off, and in the end Mr Jacobs tossed two of them towards me and said, 'Hey, young 'un, take those inside – do something useful.' That was it. I had to go in.

Fear was something I didn't like – never had – but the decision had been made for me, and I had to do it. I gripped the soft feathery pillows, held them close to my face so that if necessary I could bury it and not have to look, and walked down the front path.

I had gone but a few steps when I heard someone calling, 'Nan! Nan Hathaway!' Yes, it was my name.

I stopped and turned. There, standing by our lorry was a familiar figure. It was Sheila, my friend from school. She was grinning from ear to ear and beckoned to me.

'Look, Nan!' she called. 'That's our house – just there. We're moving in today, too.'

I dropped the pillows and ran to her. 'Sheila!' I cried.

She waved her arm. 'That's our house – number 2,' she said. 'We're going to live right by you and you're by us.'

'Fancy,' I said.

'Yeah, fancy,' she replied, and we stood beaming at each other.

Suddenly the big house didn't seem so bad – I was going to like living here, I decided.

'I'll see you later – got to go and help.'

I ran inside, forgetting the pillows.

'Mum! Mum! Guess what?'

All the stuff deposited at last inside the house and Mr Jacobs gone home, we all sighed a big sigh of relief. It hadn't rained. The chickens were in their crates in the back garden and not one had made a bid for freedom. Mr Phillips, next door to our old house, had brought a wheelbarrow full of logs and the Germans hadn't dropped any bombs on us. Life was getting better all the time. We all clomped about on the wooden floors, exploring every room, opening door after door, wide-eyed at the size of each wonder, at the big windows, at the number of fitted cupboards – in fact, at everything. Mum was delighted with the kitchen. Being the room where she undoubtedly would spend most of her time, it was a good thing that she was and I had to agree with her – it was such an improvement on the last one. There was a brand-new gas cooker with shiny brass taps like little dewdrops to turn it on and off and a gas copper! An indoor copper to boil up the whites on washday. No more standing out in the outhouse in freezing temperatures stoking the fire beneath the old one – it must have been heaven for Mum, that kitchen with the stone-flagged floor, the alcove to stand the wooden-rollered mangle in, the huge larder and broom cupboard, the high shelves right round the walls and the sink with a hot tap as well as a cold one.

In the corner of the living room was a big open-fronted cupboard, which Betty called a 'dresser'. It had shelves above a deep base cupboard and I knew instantly that Mum's cherished bits and pieces would soon fill it. The fireplace had creamy-coloured tiles round it and a polished mantelpiece above – and the room was so big! The hallway had a floor of red quarry tiles with a small cupboard for the gas and electricity meters, and the doors for the bathroom and toilet led off from here. An indoor toilet! There was another room – Mum said it was to be the 'best room' and would only be used on special occasions, like Christmas, but I wanted to live in it all the time because it had a big window that looked right down the garden to where the chickens would be kept – when Dad would build their sheds.

Up the stairs we thumped, past a long narrow window (which seemed to me to reach right up the sky) and on to the landing. This seemed to stretch away into eternity – it was so long. Five bedrooms led off from it, two to the left and two to the right and one at the far end, facing us as we stood in a huddle at the top of the stairs.

'Gosh!' said Lila.

Mum opened each door in turn. The first one on the left she said was for Susan and Pat because that would mean they were right opposite her and Dad, who were to be in the first one on the right.

Next to them was John, who was smiling happily at the thought of a room all to himself and in the front, too. Betty was to have the room next to Susan and the baby all to herself because she was 'growing up', and in the big room at the end – I held my breath (I really wanted to sleep in this room) – would be Lila and Joan in a double bed and, wonder of wonders, me in a single bed of my own! I would actually be able to wake up in the morning without a damp nightie from Susan. The bedroom itself was the whole width of the house with a window at the front and another at the back, and when we looked out of these we were over the next-door garden. It didn't seem right, Mum told Dad later – it seemed as if we were trespassing on the next house – but Dad said that ours and the house Sheila was living in were the only two in the road like that, and subsequently the houses next door were only two-bedroomed. I think it was a council experiment, but not a good one because as far as I know no other houses were built this way, and recently I was told that these extra rooms have since been included in the two-bedroomed houses, making our old house into a four-bedroomed one. We children thought it was wonderful, though, and had many an argument with the children who eventually moved into number 6, saying that because we were rich we needed part of their house. So that first night, tired and not a little irritable, we went to bed at number 8. With a bed of my very own, in that fantastic great room, with my dearest friend sleeping just two houses away, the perfumed smell of Lila's talcum powder, with which she covered herself at night, filling my nostrils, and no damp Susan, I slept well. I was very happy.

The next day while Mum stacked things in drawers and cupboards, and Dad, who had a day off to help, busied himself with the heavier jobs, Joan, John and I decided to go outside and have a look round.

'Take Sue with you,' said Mum from somewhere inside the larder.

'Oh, Mum!' whined Joan.

'She'll only get into mischief and we've got a lot to do.'

So reluctantly we dragged the unwilling Sue out into the garden with us, through the waist-high field grass to the wire-mesh fencing that marked our boundaries.

'What a long garden!' said Joan.

Our other garden had been quite large, but this one was much longer. I looked round.

'No chicken houses,' I said.

'Dad's got to build them, I suppose,' said John.

'But where are the chickens?' I looked round at the waving grasses and blue thistles.

'Over there.' John pointed.

They were still in their crates. We swooshed our way towards them.

'Poor things,' said Joan. 'I hope they've been fed.' She bent down. 'Let's let them out.'

We undid the string that held them prisoner, and with a great flurry of wings and feathers and clouds of dust they were free, squawking and clucking, unsure of their footing in the long grass. Dad heard the commotion from indoors and appeared at the back door.

'What're you doing?' he shouted. 'I've not put the coop up yet – they'll get lost!'

Sue began to cry and I tried to hide behind John.

'For goodness' sake leave things alone. Go and find something to do.'

Dad was angry, but he went back inside, and Joan said, 'Let's go and see what's over the bottom fence.'

So we trooped down the garden, leaving the hens and the cockerel to stretch their legs. Over the fence was a deep grassy field, dropping to a darker green at its lowest point, with a row of willow trees and a stream just visible to us from our vantage point on top of the fence. Beyond the stream the field swept upwards through scrubby groups of may bushes and great clumps of bramble. There were no houses anywhere, just fields.

'Cor,' said John.

'It's called a dell,' said Joan, who read a lot of books and seemed to know these things.

'Nice, isn't it?' I whispered.

Susan tried to push between us, poking the toes of her sandals into the holes in the mesh fence in an effort to climb up.

'Can't see,' she complained.

Joan lifted her up. 'See?' she asked.

Sue screwed up her eyes. 'What is it?' she asked, peering across the green expanse.

'It's a dell,' I said reverently – just in case a dell turned out to be something churchy. After all, I had never heard the word spoken before, so it could quite possibly be.

'It's just fields,' grumbled John. He had no romance in his soul at all. 'Let's go and see if anyone else is moving in.'

That turned out to be a big disappointment because the street was empty. I looked at number 2, hoping to see Sheila, but there was just a woman hanging curtains in an upstairs window – her Mum, I supposed.

'There's a man on a bike over there,' said Joan, grabbing Sue's hand. 'Let's go and see what he's doing.'

She started hurrying towards the end of the road, where there were some strangely shaped buildings, all with the same blank windows as the houses.

'Why are these houses funny?' I asked.

'They're flats.'

I couldn't see that they were in any way flat, but Joan was older so I thought she must know what she was talking about. I trudged along behind, somehow uneasy in the silence.

When we reached the wall surrounding the 'flats', we leant on our elbows and watched the man. He was peering through the windows, holding on to his bike handlebars with one hand and shading his eyes as he pressed his nose on the glass.

'What's he doing?' John whispered.

'Dunno,' said Joan.

'Do you think he's a burglar?' I hissed.

''Spect so,' said John.

'There's nothing to steal. There's no one living there,' said the clever Joan.

Then he turned and saw us and whether we unnerved him I don't know, but he took one look at the four faces on the wall and hurried off, scooting with one foot on the pedal of his bike until he was some way off then swinging his leg over the saddle and pedalling away.

'What was he doing?'

'Dunno.'

Back in the safety of our back garden Dad was having a terrible time chasing one of the hens, which had a grass snake in her beak. The poor thing was writhing and twisting about in a frantic effort to escape being the chicken's lunch, and Dad was making desperate lunges at the hen as she dodged and darted about with her prize. The others watched from a close huddle, clawking and chuckling to each other as they watched the fracas. Mum shouted to us to keep out of the way.

'It's a snake!' she shouted. 'Keep back!'

Dad made yet another lunge, missed, lurched forward again, missed again and stopped, his hands on his hips.

'Stupid blasted bird!' he said. 'The damned thing'll choke her.'

'Is it an adder, Dad?' asked John.

'No, just a grass snake. Won't hurt you, but it may hurt the silly chicken.'

'I'll get it, Dad,' shouted John, and he started towards the hen, who watched us with her little round eyes, shaking her head every now and then as the snake twisted and turned.

John's sudden movement set the other birds scurrying and flurrying in all directions; Sue, in a panic, ran and fell headlong while the chickens flapped and flew around her, frightened even more by her shrill screams.

Mum, forgetting her fear of the snake, rushed into the melee, flapping her apron and shouting, 'Go away, go away,' as she tried to haul Susan up on to her feet.

Joan stood with her hands over her eyes in case the chickens should fly near her face, and I stood beside her paralysed with fear. If there was one snake then there would probably be more; I looked round uneasily, and step by step I made my way into the house, where I made my way upstairs to the safety of my bedroom, and there I stayed until the chaos out in the garden had subsided. I just hoped that snakes couldn't climb stairs.

Dad said that that must be next on the list – getting that grass scythed down – and I was more than pleased to hear him say that. John was a bit upset though. He wanted to catch a snake to keep as a pet. I hoped Dad would hurry up. Joan whispered to me, in bed that night, that the chicken had eaten her catch and that all its guts had spilled out. I found it difficult to sleep that night because every time I closed my eyes I could see snakes with their entrails hanging out, but I was sure John would have had no trouble.

Over the course of the next few weeks the houses began to fill up, and we spent a lot of time watching the lorries coming and going, and armies of removal men trundling furniture through the different front doors. It reminded me very much of a long row of monsters all standing with their mouths wide open, being fed with chairs, tables, beds, sideboards, wardrobes and thousands of cardboard boxes.

We would stand, our hands behind our backs, enthralled by all the new faces, then run home and tell Mum, 'Number 21 opposite has got lots of kids and a budgie and a cat, and number 4 has got a horrible stuck-up girl – she put her tongue out at us – and number 12 has got their gran or someone living with them. She's about 100 years old with crinkly skin and slippers on.'

Then off we would go to nose some more.

At school we discovered that a lot of the children were now living in 'our road', and each morning the crowd that trudged off from the road grew bigger and bigger until there must have been thirty-five or so children on their way to school each morning. And that was not all of them because a few of the houses remained empty for quite a while after we had moved in. Sheila and I would stick together on the outside of the group and listen to their chatter, playing with the same crowd after school. It was nice to be with so many kids of all ages, boys and girls.

Some of the bigger children had already explored the dell, but Dad had told me I was much too small to go wandering off as we didn't know the area very well. I suspect he had also told John this, but John had explored it from end to end and said it was a magic place with lots of dark secrets.

Then one day, as Sheila and I trailed behind the gang, with our coats inside out and tied round our waists to make long dresses (Sheila and I longed to be grand ladies), she suddenly said, 'I know a short-cut,' and darted off down a rutted track beside the path.

I ran after her, trying not to trip over my coat.

'Where are we going?'

'Come on – it's all right!' she shouted over her shoulder, undoing the belt that held her coat in place as she ran.

We followed the track, Sheila haring along in front of me, down a steep incline to two tall willow trees and a stream. The path ahead of us rose again steeply, but Sheila stopped. I realised that the stream was the same one that wandered through the dell because there it was to our left in all its green mysteriousness and in the distance were the roofs of our houses.

'Come on!' Sheila shuffled down the bank to the stream, on her thick navy-blue knickers, and jumped it at the bottom.

I followed more carefully, trying to avoid the thick black mud that oozed from between the tussocks of grass.

'It smells,' I complained.

'It's a swamp,' explained Sheila. 'My dad told me. He said that swamps swallow you up and kill you.' Her face beamed at me from the far side of the water. 'You get sucked down in them – and you die.'

Panic gripped me.

'I'm not coming,' I said, turning away.

'You'll have to go back on your own.'

I looked round at the spongy ground.

'What if it sucks me?' I asked in a trembling voice.

'It won't if you do what I did,' she said. 'Just jump over here.'

I still hesitated and Sheila turned her back on me.

'Suit yourself,' she said. 'I'm going.'

That did it. The thought of being left alone in a swamp that sucked people to death gave me the courage I needed. I closed my eyes, hurtled into space and landed on firm ground on the other side. I'd done it. There was another section of boggy ground to pick our way through to the firmer ground in the long grass, and by the time we reached that we were in a sorry state. I looked down at my grey school socks and my once shiny shoes in horror. A vision of Dad's face when he saw them rose before me and my heart beat faster. Mum, too, wasn't going to be exactly happy. I almost felt the sting of Dad's hand on the back of my legs. I raised one leg and rubbed the calf. Sheila was already sitting down, peeling off her wet socks, her shoes lying beside her. She stuffed the offending articles into her coat pocket.

'I'll just put them in the wash. I'll say they are Beryl's.' Beryl was her younger sister. She scrubbed away at her legs with handfuls of grass, chattering away as if she did this sort of thing all the time. 'Good here, ain't it?' she said, screwing up her eyes as she looked up at me.

She had a mop of red-brown curls which framed her oval face, and a wide smile that showed off her square, white teeth.

I couldn't answer her. I just stared at the mess and thought of the wrath to come at home. I had not only got my school things dirty; I was actually in the dell, standing there, in defiance of Dad, with filthy legs, wet muddy socks, and shoes that were neither black nor brown – just a mud colour.

As we climbed the hill towards the road and home, John appeared at the top. He made his way down towards us, swishing his arms at the waving grass.

'Mum's looking for you,' he said, and I felt his eyes travelling over the lower half of my legs. I almost heard the gloating in his voice as he added, 'You're going to get it.'

Indoors, trying to keep my legs and feet out of sight behind the table with its long cloth, I reported to Mum.

'Nan,' she said, taking her purse from her apron pocket and a shilling from it, 'run to the shops. Joan is round there, but I forgot to ask her to get some salt.'

She handed me the money and I sped off.

My socks were beginning to look better with every step I took as they dried to a softer grey, and a piece of newspaper in a gutter served as a cleaner to remove most of the mud from my shoes – easier to shift now that the black ooze had almost powdered. My heart at last began to lift and it was almost singing by the time I found Joan.

It hadn't been a bad day at all – and I had been in the dell!

CHAPTER 3

The war had disappeared from our young minds, although I daresay the adults were having a worrying time. Then one day, while we were sitting in class and Miss Haithwaite read to us, as she always did on a Wednesday morning, the door opened and the caretaker came in carrying a long ladder.

He said, 'Excuse me, missus' to Miss and leant the ladder against a wall.

We watched, intrigued that he would dare interrupt a lesson. To our astonishment Miss didn't seem to mind at all, but rapped on her desk to regain our attention, and continued reading. He disappeared outside for a moment and came back in with some rolls of sticky brown paper; then, one by one, he put a cross on every windowpane, sticking it firmly into place. We were puzzled by all this, but pretended to be listening to the story as we watched out of the corner of our eyes, all with our own thoughts. He worked his way right round the room, doing all the glass with the same crosses. Like big kisses they were, on the bottom of a letter. Then he'd finished.

'Ta, missus,' he said in his gravelly voice, then he picked up the remains of the rolls and his ladder and struggled out of the door.

We were given no explanation of this strange behaviour and I couldn't wait to get home to tell Mum. She was in the kitchen slicing bread for tea.

'It's for the blast,' she said, without looking up from her task.

'Oh.'

I made a little hill out of a pile of breadcrumbs on the corner of the breadboard.

'Mind your fingers,' she said.

During tea the others were all talking about windows and sticky tape. It seemed that they had all been visited by men with ladders. When Betty and Lila came in, red-faced from their bike ride up from town, they said that the windows on the shops in town were also sporting big crosses of tape.

'It's for the blast,' we all chorused.

I had no idea what this 'blast' was. I only knew it was a swear word.

Next day Dad set about putting sticky tape on our big window on the stairs. Although he said that the other windows didn't need it because the panes were so small, Mum insisted that they did. I stood and watched and wondered why windows had to be treated in this way because of a swear word. Perhaps it was a worse one than I thought. I decided that I must never say it ever again.

There was a lot of talk about this time amongst us kids of a man called Hitler. I had no idea who he was, but nobody seemed to like him very much so I decided that I didn't either. They would sing funny songs about him and recite rhymes – in fact, there were drawings of him in chalk on the road and on walls, and a huge one of him on the side of a garage in the next street. He had a cross-looking face, a tiny black moustache and hair that draped across his forehead. Underneath were written the words 'Heil Hitler'. I thought that Heil must be his Christian name, because it wasn't English and Johnny Winters had told me that he was a German. I always fancied myself as a bit of an artist, so one day at school I set about drawing Heil Hitler on my slate. I thought it was a very good likeness and proudly displayed it to all my classmates; then, to my horror, I was suddenly hauled before Mrs Doughty, the headmistress, complete with slate, and severely admonished before receiving a slap on both hands. I set up such a howl. I had no idea what could cause such wrath and felt I had been unjustly punished, so I howled and howled.

I daren't tell Mum or Dad because I thought I must have done something so dreadful that I would get another hiding if they knew about it. But someone else had other ideas because one evening Dad said, 'What have you been up to, young lady?'

'Nothing,' I said.

'I heard that you had a whacking the other day because of something you drew on a slate.'

My pulses raced.

'Only a face.'

'I was told it was Hitler you drew.'

'I only drew that face on the garage round Bulan Place. I only drew Heil Hitler.' I could feel the tears starting.

Mum appeared in the doorway, wiping her hands on her apron. 'You mustn't draw him, Nan. He's a very bad man,' she said.

'Did you get the stick?' asked Dad.

'I got a smack and I don't know why!' I was shouting now, my face quite purple. 'She shouldn't have hit me. I only did a face.'

'Don't do it again,' said Dad. 'People get angry when they see his face. He's not a very nice person. He's the man that this war is all about.' His voice was softer as he tried to explain.

'I don't care. I don't!' I shouted. 'She shouldn't have smacked me. She's blasted silly.'

And I raced upstairs and flung myself on my bed, sobbing.

Later, when the tears had stopped, but the occasional sob still surfaced, I lay on my back staring up at the ceiling. I had made my little bid for independence and I had said that naughty word.

My eyes moved slowly across to the window. The 'blast' had not cracked them, so that silly sticky-tape business had been a waste of time.

'Blast,' I whispered.

No cracks.

'Blast,' this time a little louder.

Nothing.

'Blast, blast, blast!'

The panes remained intact. Why did people lie to me or not explain things? I turned over and etched Hitler's face with my finger on the wall. If only I had a piece of chalk, I'd show 'em.

A week or so later, as we sat in our nightclothes after our Friday-night baths, eating biscuits slowly so that we could stay up as long as possible, because we knew that as soon as the last mouthful had gone it would be 'up the wooden hill to Bedfordshire', there was a knock on the front door. Mum looked up from folding the damp towels.

'See who it is, Ted,' she said to Dad.

We listened eagerly – it was not often we had visitors in the evenings.

'Yes, certainly, come on in,' we heard Dad saying out in the hallway, and he ushered in a man carrying a big cardboard box.

We were immediately intrigued.

'It's Harold, Lal,' said Dad. 'He's brought our gas masks.'

'Oh, lor,' said Mum, her nose shiny and very pink from the exertion of putting us all through our ablutions. She looked decidedly worried.

'Nothing to worry about, Mrs Hathaway,' said Harold, setting the box on the floor. 'There's one for each of you in here and a couple of Mickey Mouses for the little ones.'

We pricked up our ears at the mention of Mickey Mouse and edged forward for a better view. Dad prevented us from getting too close.

'Let the man see what he's doing,' he said.

The box was opened and out came the weirdest thing I think I had ever seen. It was dark grey in colour and made of rubber with a sort of tin lid on the bottom with holes in it, and lots of straps and a little oblong window in the front. I was disappointed. It didn't look a bit like Mickey Mouse.

'You put it on like this,' said Harold, and he pulled the horrid thing over his face.

He blinked at us from behind the window. Our eyes were enormous with wonder. What was he doing?

Dad took another from the box and put it on himself. He gazed round at us. We were speechless. His eyes were all crinkled up, so we knew he must be smiling, but we couldn't think why.

Harold pulled his off.

'Come on, kids,' he said. 'Try one.' He held the object out to John. 'Here you are, John,' he said. 'You show the girls how it's done.'

John put out a tentative hand. He was unsure, but couldn't let us girls think he was afraid. He took it, looked at it, chewed fast on his mouthful of biscuit, swallowed hard and buried his face in the depths of the thing.

'It's OK.' His voice was muffled and he laughed, steaming up the visor. 'It's jolly good.' he held out his hands and walked stiffly towards Joan. 'I'm a monster,' he growled. 'G-r-r-r.'

One by one we were shown how to put them on and Dad and Harold adjusted straps as necessary so that they fitted snugly. They smelled a bit like bicycle inner tubes and if you laughed they fogged up, so we snatched them off, laughing, and wiped them clear. Then we all sat round, waggling our heads to make the trunk-like front shiver and shake, laughing at each other, mindful all the time that we were staying up past our bedtime.

'What about Susan?' said Mum, noticing the toddler watching from the safety of her hiding place behind the clothes horse.

Harold reached into the box again.

'What about this, then?'

He held up a stranger-looking object still. It was red with two round little windows like eyes and a flap that stuck out of the front.

'Mickey Mouse,' he said. 'Here, Mother,' – he handed Mum the mask – 'you put it on her.'

Mum took it from him and turned it over slowly. She glanced at Susan, who made a bid for freedom, only to be snatched by Dad.

'Oh, I couldn't,' said Mum. 'She's so little. Supposing . . .'

'Supposing what?' said Harold. 'It won't hurt her.'

'Suppose she can't breathe – she's only three.'

''Course it'll be all right. 'Course she'll be able to breathe. She breathes through this thing.'

He reached out and tweaked the flap. It looked to me like a tongue. People didn't breathe through a tongue – even I knew that. Dad took it from her and sat down, putting Susan on his lap.

With a lot of struggling and some worried little movements from Mum, Susan was finally trapped inside the thing, and Dad set her down on the mat, where she stood in her little winceyette nightie smiling round at us all, quite the little star of the evening. She was actually showing off. She soon discovered that if you snorted through the tongue it made a rude noise, and she enjoyed this so much that Dad had a job getting it away from her later. I sat and watched, wishing that I was only three so that I could have one like that instead of my smelly black thing.

There was another Mickey Mouse one in the box. I took mine off. Perhaps . . .

'This is too tight for me,' I said hopefully, my eyes on the box. Harold felt around the edges and tried it on me again.

'No,' he said, 'that's OK.'

He turned to the last one in the box. I held my breath.

'This one is for the other little one,' he said, and my heart dropped into my feet. 'Where is she?'

'She's in bed,' said Mum.

'How old?'

'Seven months.'

He put it back into the box.

'This won't do, then. There's a special one for babies. I'll bring it round tomorrow night.'

Then he'd gone, and I didn't get the other Mickey Mouse.

'Fancy Harold being an air-raid warden,' said Mum, relieving us all of our new toys and placing them on the table.

'Responsible job that,' said Dad. 'Up the wooden hill, you lot.'

'Are we going to keep them gasser masks?' asked John.

'Yes, you've got to take them everywhere you go from now on,' said Dad. He pointed to the door. 'Now, bed!'

'Why have we got to take them with us?' asked Joan.

'Because there might be gas attacks,' explained Dad. 'I won't tell you again – go to bed.'

'Because gas smells funny,' I said, pushing Joan before me through the doorway.

'Eh?'

'You can smell it when Mum doesn't strike the match quick enough. It smells awful.'

In bed, after Mum had turned off the landing light, John called to us in a hoarse whisper: 'Germans drop gas.'

'What for?'

'To kill people. Johnny Franks told me.'

'When?'

'When there's a war.'

24

'Like now?' Joan's voice trembled and I pulled the blankets up over my chin, my nose sensitive to any smell there might be.

'Yes, that's why we've got those masks, for when they drop it on us.' John's voice came through the darkness like a bringer of doom.

I disappeared beneath the covers. 'I'm going to say my prayers now,' I said.

'So am I,' said Joan.

When Harold came the following evening we all crowded round to see what he had in his box. It was a very large box and I thought how strange it was that a mask for little Pat should need such a big container.

When he opened it up Mum let out a gasp. Inside was the weirdest thing we had ever seen. It was like a big fat cocoon, with a see-through top and a pump thing on the side. Harold opened it up.

'Put baby in,' he said, turning to Mum.

'Oh, lor,' she said.

Dad picked up Pat, who smiled at him and cooed.

'Lay her in there,' said Harold, pointing to the open case.

Dad did so. Pat beamed. Harold closed the lid.

'Now you just pump and in goes the air,' he said, working the concertina thing.

Pat's face puckered. Her mouth opened and she screamed. She yelled. She kicked her legs and she screamed and screamed. The window steamed up and she disappeared from our view. Mum darted forward.

'No, no,' she cried. 'Get her out!'

'It's OK,' said Harold. 'Watch. The pumping will clear the glass.'

He pumped harder. Pat screamed louder. Harold pumped and pumped. The whole contraption rocked precariously on the table. The window cleared and steamed up again. Pat shrieked and Harold pumped. The louder she bellowed the harder he pumped. Mum's face crumpled – she was very near to tears.

'No, oh, no,' she said quietly.

'She'll be all right. She'll get used to it.' Harold was beginning to look a trifle worried himself by now. 'Here,' he said, putting Mum's hand on to the pump, 'you have a go – it's quite easy.' Pat was almost hysterical as he made his exit. 'She'll be all right,' we heard him say as Dad let him out of the front door. 'Just keep pumping.'

As soon as the door had closed behind him, Mum wrenched open the quivering capsule and lifted an equally quivering Pat from its bowels. She hugged her close and leant her cheek against the damp, dark curls.

'Please don't ever let us have to use that thing,' she whispered, her eyes tightly closed. 'Please, please.'

We were all very close to tears by now, and silently, and with no bidding, crept off to bed.

Soon everyone was walking about the streets carrying their gas masks in little cardboard boxes hung round their necks on string, or bobbing about on their backs. Mum made us all very smart cases which covered the boxes neatly and had long slim straps of the same material. Even with such a mundane thing as a gas mask there was a great deal of one-upmanship at school, each inspecting the others' cases to see which was the best. There were felt ones and knitted ones in every colour imaginable. Ours were all in a dark-brown Rexine and had our name, school and address written in Indian ink inside the flap.

I was very proud of mine because it reminded me of a grown-up handbag, although there wasn't even enough room for a hanky because it fitted so snugly round the box. I think Mum had overestimated my height a bit though because mine sort of bumped around in the region of my bottom until, with a great deal of pulling and pushing and advice from Sheila, we discovered that it could be worn high on the back with the straps going round the front of my arms and along the back of my neck. Sheila's straps weren't long enough for her to do this, so I had an extra bit of one-upmanship in this.

When we went to Sunday school, school, shopping with Mum, or for our walks on Sundays, we carried them, but out playing in the dell, on the golf links nearby, or even on the allotment with Dad, we left them behind. It didn't occur to us that we were at risk if we were just playing. It now seems strange that even our parents didn't realise this – we could have been caught out in the open at any time. If the reason was that we might break them in our rough-and-tumble games then it seemed a very high price to pay. It didn't worry us – the innocence of childhood shielded us from such thoughts and we played happily while our means of protection hung on the pegs at home with our school coats.

CHAPTER 4

One Saturday morning as a gang of us were making our way back from a game of leaping the brook on the golf links, our legs muddy and our shoes sodden, we could see, at the top of the hill that led up from the dell, on the wasteland at the end of our road, a lorry and some men.

They appeared to be unloading some stuff from the back of it, and at once we were curious. We quickened our steps, breaking into a run through the marshy grass. David Smith was first up the hill.

'Quick,' he urged us. 'Come and see.'

One by one we reached the top, puffing and panting.

'What's going on?'

'What a lot of bricks and things!'

'Building more houses, I expect.'

We had edged towards them so that we stood in a group barely ten feet away. The men, unloading slabs of concrete, bags of cement and planks of wood, eyed us apprehensively. We must have been a strange, unwholesome-looking bunch, to say the least.

There was Joan Cobb, with her short, straight blonde hair and her wellies on the wrong feet; Mick Smith, with his grey trousers reaching almost to the top of his knee-length socks, a darker patch of grey on the seat; Margaret, his sister, with her beltless navy raincoat and her skinny legs streaked with mud; Sheila (my friend Sheila) with the elbows out of her jumper and a runny nose; David, one of Mick's brothers, his straw-coloured thatch standing on end like a brush and smears of mud across his face where he constantly wiped his nose with his grubby hands; and me, with those hated black woolly stockings that Mum insisted we wore from October onwards. I hitched them up, repositioning the elastic garter that was supposed to keep them up, but never did.

'What're you doing?' I asked.

'Building.'

'No you're not – you're unloading a lorry,' Mick grinned, but the grin quickly disappeared at the scowl he received.

'Clear off, you kids,' said one of the men. 'Go home to your mothers.'

He squeaked past us with a wheelbarrow and we skipped back, only to step forward again as soon as he was clear.

'You building a house?' Sheila sniffed, wiping her nose on her sleeve. She sniffed again.

'No. Now why don't you all go home!'

We ignored their entreaties to be left in peace and stood watching until the lorry was unloaded and had rattled, bumped and squeaked its way across the rutted waste ground and disappeared off up the road, leaving the men to sort out the heaps of stuff.

'I'm 'ungry,' said David.

'Sausages for dinner,' said Mick.

And we all went home.

Mum was dishing up platefuls of stew when I walked into the kitchen. She frowned at me over the top of her glasses.

'Look at the state of you. Where the deuce have you been?'

'Playing,' I said, shuffling myself on to a chair at the table and eyeing the steaming saucepan. I hadn't realised how hungry I was.

'Where are the others?'

She put the lid back on the big black pot.

'John's down at the Jeffs',' I said, my eyes on the plate of bread in the middle of the table.

'Run and fetch him. This will be cold.'

'Oh, Mum.' I was really hungry.

'Run quick – it won't take a minute.'

The Jeffs family lived at number 26, their only son being John's best friend.

'I want my dinner,' I wailed.

'Go and fetch him, and see if he knows where Joan is.'

I grumbled and groaned, but got off my chair and went outside.

John, Mr and Mrs Jeffs and Len were standing by their front gate gazing down towards the end of the road, where I had earlier watched the men. I ran up to them.

'What's going on?' Mrs Jeffs asked.

'Dunno.' I folded my arms like she did. Something brushed my legs and I looked down to see Judy, their black spaniel, looking up at me with her golden eyes. She wagged her tail. 'Hello, Jude,' I said.

'Go and ask them.' Mr Jeffs, tall, thin and bony, nudged his son in the back.

'Nar, I don't want to.' Len reddened, his face twitching with a nervous tic.

'I'll go,' said John.

'No you won't – it's dinner time,' I said, but he had already set off at a leggy run. 'He'll get it,' I said, and went back home to report on his disobedience. I didn't care if his dinner went cold. I was hungry.

When he did eventually arrive for dinner we had all eaten and his was waiting for him with a saucepan lid on the top. The news he had to tell was so exciting (but I couldn't see why) that he didn't even get a ticking-off!

'It's shelters they're making,' he said between forkfuls of food. 'Great big ones, for all of us to get in.' He shovelled in a piece of dumpling. 'For when the bombs drop on us.'

'Who told you that?' Mum sat down heavily on a chair at the end of the table.

'Them men did.' Down went another load of vegetables. 'It's going to be huge.' John's eyes widened, and he chewed faster. 'Everyone's gotta get inside.'

'There are hundreds of people in the world. How can we all get in?' I asked.

'Not everyone in the *world*, stupid,' said John.

'Who, then?' I wondered about all the Chinese people and the black people.

'Us lot – our street,' said John, breaking yet another piece of bread. He looked at me as if I were mad. 'Stupid,' he repeated.

I couldn't wait to tell Sheila. I loved to be the bearer of news, and within minutes I was waiting, fidgeting from foot to foot, outside her back door. She took such a long time over her dinner! Eventually the door opened and her sister, Brenda, came out and took her bike from where it leant against the wall.

'Hello, Nan,' she said. 'Have you heard about the shelters?'

I wasn't the bringer of excitement after all.

The afternoon was spent watching the men, but it was a bit boring as all they seemed to be doing was tying bits of string round little wooden pegs in the ground, waving their arms about and arguing, so we went home for tea still not able to believe that they were going to make anything that could protect a whole street-ful of people from bombs. But before very long, there it was: a long building with a flat roof and doors hidden away behind a half-wall. When we peered inside, if the men had left the door open, it was so dark we couldn't see anything.

'Black as the devil's nutting bag,' said Sheila.

'I don't like it,' I said.

''Orrible,' said Margaret.

'Spooky,' said Joan.

More of these shelters sprang up on the corners of other streets, and even in the playground at school. We couldn't climb on the school ones, but they made excellent playgrounds round the streets and we clambered on to the flat roofs and played ball up against the vast walls. The insides remained a mystery only to be revealed when one morning a whistle sounded in school and we had to file silently and quickly out, across the playground and into the shelter. Oh, the excitement! Beyond the doors were long slatted benches all along the walls and down the middle. Tiny yellow lights were dotted along the entire length, giving an eerie light, but enough to see by. Inside, our whispering increased to a babble, which echoed strangely until we were silenced and told that lessons would continue in there. However, it soon became clear that it was not possible to conduct lessons because that would mean having to bring all our books and slates and a blackboard in, so we had stories read to us.

There wasn't a real raid on during this exercise, but the thrill of it all was exhilarating and we enjoyed every minute of it.

The next thing to appear on the home scene were the 'static' tanks. They sprang up like mushrooms on street corners and spare bits of ground. Round concrete tanks, they were, filled with water and covered with wire netting. Dad warned us not to climb up to see in or we might fall in and drown, but it didn't take us long to discover that if you leant your bike against the side and stood on the saddle it was possible to push your hand under the wire and float things – leaves, matchboxes, bits of wood – all tearing about on the surface. There was a constant shipping line on its insect-infested water. We held races, blowing our vessels with rounded apple-red cheeks, laughing and squealing, and not without a little cheating with currents created by surreptitious splashing. It usually ended with a heated argument or a well-aimed stone on an opposing craft.

* * * * *

'What's rations, Mum?' Joan looked up from her drawing.

We were seated round the table, Joan, John and I, with our paintboxes, Betty sewing and Lila writing a letter. Mum sat by the fire with a great pile of darning on the floor by her feet.

'Sharing food,' said John, concentrating on his picture.

'It means that everyone gets a fair share of food when it's scarce,' said Betty.

'That's what the ration books are for,' said Mum, screwing up her eyes as she threaded a needle. 'Coupons for this, coupons for that.'

She pulled the length of grey wool through and licked her fingers to knot the end.

'Are them static tanks for water, in case that gets scarce?' I asked.

Mum laughed. 'Goodness, no.' She pulled another holey sock over the wooden mushroom. 'They're for fighting fires.'

'In the case of an air raid and bombs dropping and setting things alight,' said Betty, 'the firemen use the water in them to put it out.'

I thought of all the rubbish in the one opposite. If they used hosepipes they would most certainly get all bunged up.

'Have I had all my rations this week?' asked Joan, licking the end of her pencil.

Joan was always hungry.

'It doesn't work like that,' said Mum, and she went on to explain how the system worked, the grocer taking out coupons for everything Mum bought or marking the books so that we had our share and there would be enough for everyone. I began to understand the little black folder that she carried whenever we went to the shops. Inside were the books, grey, blue and green – one for each of us. I decided that it was very fair, and hoped that my blue book never got lost or I might starve.

'There's enough food on rations for us all, but I'm glad of the stuff from the allotment and garden and the eggs the chickens give us. I don't know how other families without those manage, I'm sure.' Mum took the sock from the mushroom, folded it and laid it on the arm of her chair. 'Go and put the kettle on, Bet,' she said. 'Let's have some cocoa.'

We knew that was the signal to pack up our things and get ready for bed.

'Dad's thinking of getting some ducks,' said John. 'I heard him telling old Piggy Lee.'

'*Mr* Lee,' said Mum.

'What for?' I asked.

'To eat.'

John put his pencils back in their box and swung the lid shut.

'Eat ducks?'

I was appalled at this. Ducks were lovely little things, all yellow and fluffy. You couldn't eat ducks!

'Got to,' said John. 'You've got to eat anything you can get hold of in wartime.'

In the warmth of my bed I thought about eating ducks. The idea was awful. I had eaten chicken, but never in a month of Sundays would I eat a duck. This war was suddenly becoming abhorrent to me. Houses burning down, bombs dropping on people, gas falling on us, and now we were expected to eat little darling fluffy yellow ducklings. No wonder I got a whack for drawing that awful Heil Hitler.

Of course this talk of food shortage caused great concern to us as we had always had more than enough to eat. We couldn't imagine what life would be like without our usual roast meat on a Sunday, our shepherd's pie on Monday, made from the leftovers of the joint, the succulent rissoles on Tuesdays, toad-in-the-hole on Wednesdays, rabbit stew on Thursdays, fish on Fridays and either a casserole or sausages and mash on Saturdays. Teatime always meant a cake, Victoria sponges on Sundays filled with home-made jam (or, if Auntie Enid and Uncle Sid arrived, with buttercream); jam tarts, fairy cakes or rock cakes during the week. There would also be great trays of bread pudding, heavy with sultanas, or apple pies, or rhubarb tarts, or baked apples filled with brown sugar and chopped dates. We certainly had an excellent range of food. In the bottom of the larder stood a large round stone bowl full of eggs, each one carrying the date it was laid; and as the hens supplied us every day there were always fresh new-laid ones for eating and the older ones for cooking. They were kept in strict rotation. Whoever collected the eggs took the stub of pencil hanging on a string inside the larder and carefully marked the shell, took out the ones in the crock, laid in the fresh ones and replaced them on top. Dad was very strict about the eggs.

'An egg is a meal,' he would say. 'There's not much you can't do with an egg.'

The thought that all this lovely fare might be denied us made us apprehensive and we vowed that we would always be very careful not to waste anything. I didn't dare tell Dad or Mum that John was still secreting his crusts under the table on the ledge where the extra leaf fitted in. I thought he was very wicked, but he was my brother, and although he was wasting food my loyalty held. It wasn't until Mum was polishing the lino under the table, having decided to move the furniture round, that she happened to look up and saw all those mildewy scraps. When we came in from school there on the table, instead of a plate of bread and butter, was a tea plate holding them.

We stared and shuffled our feet.

'Yes, you may look ashamed,' said Mum. 'Who's the guilty one? Or are you all guilty?' She pointed to our chairs. 'Sit down, and before we start I want to know who put these under the table.' She frowned at us over her specs. 'Own up.'

I glanced at John, who had gone very red.

'Wasn't me,' I said.

'And it wasn't me,' said Joan.

'John?' Mum asked.

John said nothing.

'I somehow thought it was you,' said Mum. 'Well, my lad, you can have them for your tea.'

Joan gasped, 'He can't eat them – they're green.'

'He put them under there, and we have told you and told you that food must not be wasted. That is a terrible waste.' Mum turned to John. 'So sit yourself down and start eating, young man.'

Food must be very scarce if John was having to eat mouldy bread. I held my breath. I couldn't bear the thought of him having to put the green, dusty things in his mouth. I looked at him and saw that his eyes had filled with tears. He slowly got on to his chair and pulled the plate towards him and picked up one of the crusts. He blinked his tears away and slowly opened his mouth. I watched in horror as the obnoxious thing travelled to the opening.

'No,' I shouted, 'don't, John – it'll poison you.'

Still it continued without a tremor.

I dashed round the table – 'Don't! Don't!' – and dashed it from his hand.

He burst into tears.

Mum was beside him in a flash. She put her arms round him. 'All right, son,' she said, 'don't cry. I just wanted you to see how important it is that nothing is wasted. There are people in other countries that haven't seen a loaf of good bread for a long time, and people without homes and people who have lost their entire families. We must be grateful for everything we have and not take things for granted.' She wiped John's eyes with her apron. 'You do see, don't you?'

He nodded, sniffed and wiped his nose with the back of his hand.

'OK,' she said. 'Now I'll go and get your teas.'

We had listened intently to her words, but not long afterwards I found more crusts on the ledge; but I didn't dare tell.

It was about this time that the scrumping started. There on the trees over at White's farm and in the Franks' garden, and just round the corner in the Horwoods' garden were apples, plums, greengages, damsons and pears. Food! We had a Victoria plum tree on the allotment, and gooseberry bushes and blackcurrants as well as all the vegetables, but these were extras. Firstly we snatched an occasional apple or pear on our way to school, but when Mum happened to say one day that she had had to make another jam tart because the plums weren't quite ready from the allotment we decided that a few fruits from the trees around us would help. John, as usual, was the first. He came in one evening with his jumper all knobbly down the front, walked over to the table, pulled the bottom of it away from his body and out rolled six or seven green apples. They rolled about on the cloth and he beamed round at us all. Mum put down her sewing.

'What's this, then?' she asked.

'Apples,' said John, proudly.

'I can see that,' she said. 'Where did you get them?'

'A tree.'

'What tree?'

'An apple tree.'

'Whose tree?'

'They were growing on an old tree in a field.'

'What field?'

'On the farm.'

'White's?'

'Yes, only this tree is on wasteland that they don't use.'

'Are you sure?'

'Yes.' He screwed up his face. 'They're a bit sour. All the kids are getting them. No one wants 'em.'

'Well, I suppose it's all right, then.' Up came the sewing again and we knew that everything was. 'Put them out in the kitchen, then.'

That was the opening for us all to bring home 'gifts' for the kitchen. Every evening, while the light lasted, we crept commando-style through long grass and bushes and systematically stripped all the outer trees in Mr White's orchard. Pockets, pixie hats and jumpers bulging, we transported fruit home. Mum began to get a bit suspicious after the fourth or fifth time, so we decided to distribute the ill-gotten gains around a bit. There were never such grateful neighbours.

We knocked on the doors and handed over the fruit with 'Oh, we've got too many on the allotment. Dad said would you like these?'

Sometimes we would get a penny or two for our trouble.

We had plum pies, apple dumplings, stewed apples, baked apples, pears and custard. This was living. Mum didn't seem quite so worried about the supply, even though John had said that the apples were from an old tree no one wanted. She didn't ask how or where we got greengages, pears and plums as well.

One night we nearly got caught. Sheila, Joy Hillier, Margaret Pollard, Mick Smith, Johnny Winters, John and I were all in the orchard that ran alongside the allotments. This was an entirely new venue and the pickings were bountiful. We had filled everything we had brought with us and were just about to leave, because it had suddenly got very dark, when we heard a shout. Coming along the track we could just make out the figure of a man.

'He's got a gun,' shouted Johnny Winters, and we took off at a frantic run. Reaching the five-barred gate at the end of the lane, we didn't stop to open it. Straight over the top we scrambled, pushing and grabbing at each other in our efforts to get away. Only then did we look back. The man was waving a stick in the air and shouting something we couldn't quite make out, although we knew it wasn't very nice. Then we realised that John wasn't with us. Panic again gripped us. He was somewhere back there with that awful man. The man would catch him and probably give him a good beating with that stick. We didn't know what to do.

'If we call out something to him, he'll chase us,' Mick said in a hoarse whisper.

'Don't be barmy,' said Sheila. 'What if he catches us?'

'He'll get John, anyway.'

'He can't catch all of us,' Mick said. 'He can only chase one at a time if we all split up.'

I glanced back along the dark lane. The thought of that angry man hot on my heels didn't appeal at all.

'Let's go and get my dad,' I said.

'Dafty!' said Joy. 'How are you going tell him what we were doing?'

'I must get him.' My voice trembled. 'John'll be murdered.'

The dark outline of the man was just visible to us. He still waved his stick in the air.

'I'm off,' said Johnny Winters, and took off into the dark.

Joy followed on his heels and so did Margaret.

'Me too,' said Mick. He grabbed my arm. 'Come on.'

Sheila was already running, so with one last look, my legs like jelly, I, too, ran.

It wasn't until I reached home that I realised I had left my booty by the five-barred gate. I was very miserable when I went to bed. John had still not come home and Dad was about to set off to look for him.

'Where is he?' he asked me.

'Dunno.'

'You were with him earlier – I saw you both up by Joy's.'

'He went off.' I didn't like telling lies, but sometimes they did seem necessary.

The back door opened and John walked in.

'Come in, son,' said Dad. 'I was just about to come looking.'

'Sorry.' John glared at me. 'Got held up.'

Later, he came into my room and stood at the end of my bed.

'Why did you lot run?' he said.

Joan lifted her head from the pillow. 'What's been going on?' she asked.

'We was scrumping and a man came,' I said.

'Bloody nasty he was,' said John.

'Don't swear.'

'Did he get you?' I sat up, excited but scared.

'Naw.' He scratched his stomach, ruffling his pyjama jacket. 'I was up that tree and he stopped right underneath me.'

'Gosh.'

'He was yelling about getting his dogs to chase you, so I just kept very quiet. When I saw you all running away I got a bit scared, but then I thought if he was to chase you lot I could get out of the tree.'

'But he didn't chase us,' I said.

'I know. I just had to sit still and wait till he went off.'

'You kids are going to get into real trouble one of these days.' Joan's voice came from under her blankets. 'Don't ask me to help you when you're all in gaol. If Jesus is watching He won't be very pleased.'

'He wouldn't be very pleased if you didn't help us, so there,' said John. Then to me he said, 'Did you get many apples?'

'I left 'em behind,' I said mournfully.

'Silly cat,' he said.

'Did you?'

'Not many.'

'Oh.'

As he made his way back to his own room, Joan said, 'Serves you right if you *do* get caught. Now I'm going to say my prayers, and I think you'd better say yours an' all.'

But our experience did not deter us, and night after night we were out. Pears, apples and gooseberries came flooding in. In the end Mum said that we must stop. She said that no one these days would leave good fruit on trees and bushes to rot and she said that although she couldn't prove anything she had just the slightest inkling that things were not all above board so she would be very grateful if we would stop. Personally I think she knew all along what we were up to, but was glad of the extra food, and I think it got a bit embarrassing after a while because she had always told us it was wrong to steal. What made things worse was Dad coming home one Sunday from the allotment and raving that someone had practically cleaned up our Victoria plum tree. It wasn't us. We felt very indignant about it. How dare some thieving person help themselves to our fruit! Joan said that we must ask God for forgiveness in Sunday school, and we said we would if we could be sure that the plum pincher was also.

* * * * *

'No walks this Sunday – I shall need all the help I can get.'

Dad was putting on his jacket to go to work. He was on a later shift this week, so it was eight o'clock in the morning and we were all seated round the table eating breakfast.

'What for, Dad?' asked John.

'I'm building the shelter in the garden.' He put his cap on his head and picked up his lunch bag, checking to make sure it was fastened properly. 'It's being delivered sometime today and I need you all to help dig out the hole.' He kissed Mum on the cheek and made for the door. 'Saturday, too, so don't get making any arrangements.'

The door closed behind him and we stared silently at each other.

I was first to speak: 'It'll have to be a big hole.' I pictured the shelters at the end of the road.

'Huge,' said John.

'Our garden will be all used up,' said Joan.

I told Sheila about it on our way to school.

She scoffed, 'Don't talk daft, Nan Hathaway. You won't get a shelter in your garden. What about all your spuds and carrots and things? And where will your chicken sheds go?'

'My dad said so, and he don't tell lies,' I defended. 'We're all going to help do it.'

When we got home, there against the wall at the back of the house leant a load of curved silvery wrinkly iron sheets.

'Is that it?' I asked Joan.

She studied it for a while.

'Suppose so,' she said.

'Don't look like a shelter to me. Just a load of old tin.'

But, yes, that was it.

All weekend we dug – at first with great rushes of energy, squeals of delight and happy exchanges of conversation. By teatime on Saturday there were squabbles and shoves and pushes, arguments over the shovels, and lots of 'Dad, he's not doing it properly' and 'Get out of the way.' Sunday was worse. No one wanted to do it, really. Dad was getting more than a little annoyed as we got in the way and grumbled at every spadeful.

Then, at last, he said, 'OK, looks like we've done it.'

With great gushing sighs of relief we flung down the tools. There was an enormous square hole in the ground. Mum came out to look.

'Big, isn't it?' she said, peering down into the depths.

'Got to be to take that lot,' said Dad, pointing to the iron sheets.

We hoped there would be no air raids during the following week because there wouldn't be much protection from a big hole in the ground, but we had to wait until the following Saturday before it could be completed. There was a raid on the Tuesday night and, as usual, we were dragged from our nice warm beds, wrapped in blankets and stuffed in the little cupboard under the stairs. There was not much room in there for all of us, but we managed to doze amidst the tangle of arms and legs; and usually when the all-clear sounded we were so sleepy that we could hardly remember going back to bed. Apart from searchlights raking the sky with their long tapering fingers, there was no activity outside during any raid and we began to wonder what all the fuss was about. It hardly seemed worth the disturbance, but Mum explained that bombs were falling everywhere else and we should think ourselves very lucky that we lived where we did. Just as we were getting complacent about the sirens sounding, the guns on the marsh, down in Cowley, opened up. With great crumping booms they hammered away one evening and we couldn't get into our little cupboard quickly enough. We were very scared, so Betty kept us all calm by making finger shadows in the candlelight and drew cartoon characters all over the walls. Mum was very grateful to her – I reckon she must have been, because normally we were never allowed to scribble on the walls, even if they were just walls inside the meter cupboard. I often wonder what the people who moved into the house after us made of all the faces and animals and fairies and elves on the walls, because Dad wouldn't paint over them.

The following weekend Dad and Mr Rolfe, from number 4, completed the shelter. It was almost completely submerged apart from its rounded top, and this they covered with soil and, eventually, grass. It had a wooden ladder to get down into it, and benches along each side inside. Shelves along each inside wall held candles, tinned food and a big water container. We thought it very cosy, although it smelled a bit funny, all earthy and strangely metal-y. We were warned that it was not a play shed and there would be terrible chastisements if we were caught down there. I must admit that Sheila and I often crept down into its dark interior and sat on the benches whispering together, enjoying the thrill of sheer defiance. I kept wishing that the siren would go, but it was almost a week before it did. Oh, the thrill of having our very own shelter.

We sat huddled together, just our eyes showing over the top of our blankets, watching the flickering shadows playing up and down and from side to side on the corrugated walls. Dad stood, much to Mum's consternation, at the top of the ladder, watching the sky. We prayed that the Germans wouldn't see him.

After the raid, as we were shepherded back into the house, John said, 'What did you see, Dad?'

'Nothing much. A few planes went over and the searchlights picked them out, but they were ours.'

I trailed behind, trying not to trip over my blanket.

'What if they had been Germans, Dad?'

'Our boys would just shoot 'em down,' said Dad. He held the back door while we all passed through. 'Come on, Lila,' he said. 'Hurry up.'

'If our boys shot them down they'd fall on us, wouldn't they?' asked Lila, her white rag curlers bobbing.

'That's one of the reasons for the shelter,' said Dad.

'Gosh, I'm glad we've got one,' said Joan.

'So'm I,' I said.

'No one's more thankful than me,' said Mum. She hoisted the sleeping Pat up into a more comfortable position on her hip. 'Take Susan up, Ted.'

Dad picked up little Susan, her eyes large and dark with sleepiness.

'Yes, thank goodness for the old Anderson,' he said.

'The what?' asked Betty.

'The Anderson – that's what that shelter is, an Anderson.' Dad reached up with his free hand and slid the bolt into place on the door. 'Bed, now.'

'Why is it called that?' asked John.

'After the man who invented it, I suppose,' said Dad.

I went to sleep, drifting into the warmth of a soft mattress and pillow.

'The shelter's called Mr Anderson,' I mused.

* * * * *

I couldn't understand why everyone didn't have one. The grass on the top made a lovely sunbathing place, and the dark musty inside was wonderful as a place to whisper secrets to Sheila. In fact there was only one other in the entire street. Mr Wheeler at number 20 built one. I was a bit jealous when I heard from his daughter Beryl that he was digging a hole.

'It won't be as good as ours,' I said spitefully.

Mr Anderson was the best shelter in the whole wide world.

CHAPTER 5

The hedge moved. I was sure it did. I stopped in my task of egg-collecting, lowered the lid of the nesting box with its grey roofing-felt covering and stared. The bush moved again, barely perceptibly this time.

I moved along to the next box and raised the lid slowly, watching out of the corner of my eye. Rustle. Rustle. I turned sharply and saw a face peering at me from the green of the privet hedge. A small, pale face it was with dark, lank hair like a frame. I moved closer. It withdrew. I stopped. Yes, there it was again. I could see now that it belonged to a girl of about my own age.

'Hello,' I said.

'Shh!' A grubby finger came up to her mouth.

'What are you doing under there?' I asked.

She was on the far side of the fence in Mrs Lanning's garden. The wide hazel eyes with their thick black lashes were like those of a frightened rabbit. I stooped lower to see her better.

'What are you doing?' I enquired again.

''Iding.'

'Who from?'

''Er.' She inclined her head in the direction of Mrs Lanning's house.

I was curious. Mrs Lanning was a very nice lady.

'Why?' I asked.

'I wanna go 'ome.'

'Why don't you go, then?'

'Can't. I gotta stay 'ere. We ain't got no 'ouse no more.'

'Oh.'

'Don't you tell no one where I am.' Her voice was threatening.

''Course I won't,' I said, but I stepped backwards, unsure now. 'What's your name?'

It was an order, so I answered, 'Nan. Nan Hathaway.'

A movement by our back door made the face withdraw again into its green safety. Dad had emerged from the kitchen.

'Come on,' he shouted down the garden to me. 'Where the dickens have you got to?'

'Just coming,' I answered.

'Don't you tell no one.' The bush spoke in a gruff whisper.

'I said I won't and I won't,' I answered. I went back to the bowl of eggs and picked it up. 'What's your name?'

'Shan't tell yer.'

Back in the kitchen I helped Dad pencil the date on to each egg, and we put them in the crock, carefully sorting out the ones with yesterday's date on them to make sure they would be used in strict rotation. I kept thinking of the girl in the privet hedge. What on earth could have happened to make her so scared? Suddenly, next door erupted into the most horrendous shrieks and shouts and Dad looked out of the window.

'What the blazes is going on in the Lannings'?' he said.

I stood on tiptoe to see Mr Lanning, a tiny bald-headed man, was trying to coax someone to him. The someone was the girl. She screamed at him and stamped her foot.

'Come on, dearie,' he was saying. 'We want to help you. Don't be scared.'

She looked scared all right. Even from our window we could see that she was deathly white and crying bitterly. Dad went out to see if he could help and I followed on his heels, not wanting to miss anything. Mrs Lanning, a buxom lady with neatly permed hair, was standing by her back door with her hands over her cheeks, looking extremely worried.

'What's the trouble?' asked Dad.

'Oh, Mr Hathaway, it's this evacuee girl. They brought her to us today and we can't get her to come indoors. She's so frightened, poor mite. I don't think she understands that we want to help.'

'Where is she from?' asked Dad.

'London, poor dear.' Mrs Lanning's eyes were moist. 'Bombed out, they were. Her whole family have come down here to Oxford, but she has been separated from them until the council can find somewhere for them all to go. I think all her brothers and sisters are split up. Oh, I do wish she would come to us.'

Dad climbed over the fence into their garden and the girl made a rush for the safety of the bushes again, screaming as she ran. She looked like a hare chased by hounds. I felt a pang of pity for her. I desperately wanted to help her. I, too, clambered over the fence.

'Where's Mrs Hathaway?' asked Mrs Lanning. 'She should be good with kids with all your lot.'

'Shopping,' said Dad. 'She'll be back soon, though. She might be able to help.'

He started slowly down the path to where the poor, harassed Mr Lanning was standing, his arms hanging by his sides in defeat. I watched the bushes carefully for signs of movement, but saw none. Then, slowly, I walked towards Dad and Mr Lanning, straight on past them and on down to the privets. There I could see a grubby pair of skinny legs sticking out and hear stifled sobs. I crouched down and peered in, moving aside a twig or two so that I could actually see the girl. Her eyes were red with weeping, and her pale, oval face was streaked with dirt. She stared at me for a second or two and I stared back.

'I didn't tell,' I said.

She scowled. 'Don't care if you did. I'm not going in that 'ouse.' She jerked a thumb to indicate which one.

'Why not?'

'I wanna go back 'ome. I want me mum.'

'I think you're only going to stay with Mr and Mrs Lanning for a little while, then they will find you a house so you can all be together.'

'It's not like London. It's all posh in there. I don't like it.'

Mrs Lanning's home was, I had to admit, much better than most in the street. She had a large red carpet in her living room and little polished tables with plants on them. She had lace curtains at most of the windows and always a white tablecloth, while we only had a white one at Christmas when one of Mum's sisters came to visit from Croydon. I wouldn't have minded living with Mrs Lanning at all.

'But she is very nice, Mrs Lanning,' I said, 'and you'll have Jean and her big sister to play with.'

'You mean that fat girl and that stuck-up one with all the curly 'air? Huh – they won't wanna play with me.'

I had to accept that. I wouldn't play with either of them either. They just didn't play the sort of games we played. In fact, they didn't play at all. Once home from school they sat in the garden, reading, or stayed in. Mum said that she wished we were more like them – they never seemed to get dirty.

'But *I* would. I would play with you. I'm only next door.'

I must have sounded as if I meant it because she lifted her head and studied me.

'Would you?'

'Yeah, 'course I would.' I stood up. 'Come on out and see. Everything's all right – honest.'

It took just a little more coaxing, but eventually she crawled out and shakily walked with me towards her new guardians. I could have a good look at her now, at her faded summer dress with the hem hanging down at the back and at the little grey cardigan several sizes too small. She looked awfully grubby, and I wondered if Mrs Lanning would mind her having a bath in that spotless bathroom.

'This is Anne,' said Mrs Lanning, her pudgy cheeks lifting as she smiled. 'We're going to get along fine, aren't we, dear?'

The girl scowled. 'Annie,' she corrected. 'My name's Annie.'

Annie became my second-best friend. The first of the 'Vackies' in the street.

* * * * *

'I don't like these Vackies.' John flung down his jacket and flopped on to the old red horsehair sofa. 'They're 'orrible.'

Joan flew to their defence: 'They are all right,' she said. 'You must remember that they have lost their houses and all their toys and things. We have to be kind to them.'

'You've been listening to the teachers. That's what they say.

Well, I don't like them.'

He hooked one shoe off with the toe of the other and it fell with a crash on to the lino. The other one was more difficult because he hadn't the heavy leather to help, only a woolly sock.

'They're OK,' I said. 'We've got a lot in our class and Miss said that we must look after them.'

'They can jolly well look after themselves,' said John. 'They're a load of bullies.'

'Oh, I see,' said Joan: 'one of them bashed you up.'

'I bashed him good and proper,' he said, struggling with the other shoe, the laces of which seemed to have several knots in them.

'What for? Why did you fight him?' I asked.

'He said that Oxford people were stuck-ups.'

'He didn't!'

'He said that we were all scaredy-cats and couldn't knock the skin off a rice pudding.'

I wasn't sure that anyone would want to, unless they didn't like nutmeg, and John had bashed someone for it, so I turned my attention to my drawing. The conversation was getting a bit beyond my intelligence.

Dad gave us a lecture that evening about getting involved with the Vackies, and said that he would not tolerate people coming to the door with any complaints – this with a stern look at his only son, who sat hunched in the corner of the sofa, his arms folded, his chin low on his chest. Betty and Lila came home from work with stories of girls and boys working with them who had lost parents in the bombing of London – not just their homes, but their mums and dads, grans and grandfathers. We listened open-mouthed. War was evil. I made a mental note to be extra-kind to all Vackies.

At school next day there was a new face next to me in class – a girl with dark hair and almond-shaped eyes. I thought her very pretty and her name was Valerie. Valerie – how lovely that sounded compared to 'Nan'! I thought it was the best name ever. She did very neat writing and spoke quite posh, although there was still a touch of the same accent as Annie had. It sounded so different with Valerie though, probably because she sounded her aitches, while Annie never did. I found myself quite overawed by this perfect new person and found myself saying Valerie said this and Valerie said that all the time, which, on reflection, must have really cheesed poor Sheila off. But it has to be said, it was always Valerie's hand that went up first when Miss asked a question in class. Valerie was a clever girl.

Then, one day, as we spilled out at the end of the day, someone snatched my rain hat and I spun round to see my heroine hurl it right up into the top of the fir tree by the school gates. It hung there totally out of reach like a dead bat while Valerie and her group of Vackie friends stood round cackling like a load of witches as Sheila and I tried in vain to dislodge it with stones. I have never hated anyone so much, after all the adoration I had showered her with! Then we were saved. Out of the boys' gates came Sheila's brother, Keith, my brother, John, and Mick Smith. They summed up the situation very quickly and chased the girls down the road, screaming, yelling, shouting. It was wonderful to watch and worth the telling-off I got for losing my rain hat (which, as far as I know, is still at the top of that tree) to see those horrid girls put to flight in such a way. Although I still had to sit next to the wretched Valerie in class, I didn't ever speak to her again and I hated her cockiness and the way Miss said things like 'Good girl, Valerie' and 'Well done, Valerie.' It made me positively sick. Valerie Lucas had become a pain. Sheila, of course, was delighted that she was number one on my list again, and whenever we squabbled she would remind me of how I had been taken in by stuck-up Vackies who were 'only too ready to knock the likes of us down'.

We had many upsets with these children from London, when I think back. The boys were all very tough little characters and our boys usually sported a black eye or a bloody nose from one or more of them. They were not used to the more gentle ways of the 'bumpkins', as they called us, and constantly ribbed us about the way we spoke. We didn't think we were *that* countrified, although the Oxford accent (and I don't mean the university one) was a bit broad.

There was one London family that moved into one of the empty houses in our street, that consisted of two women, an old lady and several assorted children. There were no men there, so we assumed that the husbands must be in the army or something. Anyway, this crowd were the roughest lot we had ever seen. They seemed very poor, with hardly a change of clothes, and the house seemed void of any furniture. Mum would look across the road at the house and say, 'Poor things' and 'I do feel so sorry for them.' But she forbade us to have anything to do with them. Indeed, they had only been there for a couple of days before our local bobby on his bike called there.

'Oh, lor,' said Mum, because to have a policeman call was terrible.

We all hid behind the curtains and watched him in animated conversation at the front door with one of the women, who waved her arms about and was obviously arguing with him.

'See what I mean?' said Mum. 'I don't want you to go near those children. If I ever see you over there at that house, you'll be in for it.'

I was intrigued by this houseful. There were twin boys slightly younger than I, and a girl of about thirteen who wore make-up when she came home from school. There were two little girls, one of whom had a deformed arm, which hung by her side and was completely paralysed. The other had a tangled mass of light-brown hair that looked as if it hadn't been washed for months, and she swore. She could not have been more than nine years old, but she never finished a sentence without 'bloody' or 'bleeding' or 'bastard' in it somewhere. We were horrified. To say such words was more than we would ever dare, although some of the boys in our gang had been known to say 'bugger' in times of dire necessity.

There was also a baby – a poor pathetic little thing who crawled around outside getting filthy. Its nappy was always soaking wet and its nose was always running and in its mouth, almost as if it had grown there, was a big brown rubber dummy. In all the years they lived there I don't ever recall seeing that baby without that horrid great thing hanging from its mouth.

The other Vackies in the street and from the surrounding houses of other roads in the vicinity didn't seem to have much to do with them, and we all got a great deal of abuse from them – especially from the older girl. She had a bike, albeit a man's bike with the crossbar cut off, and she would ride as close as she could to our hopscotch or our whips and tops, daring us to say something. She would put out her foot and kick our 'slider' straight off the chalked squares, then stop on the other side of the road, waiting for a comment. We knew it was more than we dared do, to open our mouths, so one of us would quietly retrieve it and we played on, aware of her cold eyes watching for a false move.

Then, casually, one of us would say, 'I've had enough of this game. Let us go and play in my garden,' and, of course, everyone else would readily agree, so the game was abandoned and we retreated to the safety of someone's backyard.

Unfortunately, there was no room at our school for Annie, so she had to go to The Poplars. This was a temporary schoolhouse opened especially to take the overspill caused by the arrival of so many kids from London. It was some way away from where we lived, so every day, after school, Sheila and I would report to Mum that we were home, then start the long trek to meet Annie. There was some jealousy between Sheila and Annie – they didn't get on as well as I had hoped – but I think it was just because Annie tended to look on me as her own property for the simple reason that I had been the first to show her any sort of friendship just at the time when her world had fallen apart. She would link arms with me as soon as we met up and chatter away about her day and what she was doing at the Lannings'.

One particular day she was in a jubilant mood. She came running towards us waving her arms in delight about something.

Sheila caught hold of my sleeve. 'I reckon she's coming to our school,' she said quietly. 'I don't want her to.'

I thought it would be nice to have Annie there and said so, but it was nothing to do with school.

'Guess what!' Annie was shouting long before she reached us. 'My mum and dad have been given that empty 'ouse over the road. We're all going to live there. My teacher told me. She said she 'ad a letter or som'ink. It was to say they are all coming – Mum, Dad, everyone.'

Sheila kicked at a stone. 'All your family?' she asked.

'Yeah, me mum and all me bruvvers and sisters – good, ain't it?

I can't believe it.' Her eyes were shining and she drew the back of her hand across her nose. 'Honest to Gawd, I can't wait.'

She was right. The very next day a van pulled up outside number 31 and out got a short, fat woman, followed by a tall, thin man carrying a big bundle. Then a pretty girl of about seventeen, a boy about John's age and finally a little girl of five or so. Sheila and I stood by my front gate and watched until Mum tapped on the window and told us to get a move on or we'd be late. We walked backwards to the end of the road not to miss a thing, then a car pulled up and out got a small man with a clipboard under his arm. He unlocked the house and the newcomers all disappeared inside.

I felt sad that Annie had not been there to see them arrive, but she had a long walk to school, and had already left. Sheila seemed surprisingly happy, which perplexed me – until playtime.

We were sitting on the steps by the lavatories, chalking patterns on our window-breaker tops when she said, 'Now Annie's family has moved into that house over the road you won't have to be friends with Annie, will you?'

'Why not?' I asked, licking my thumb and wiping off a zigzag line that hadn't quite gone where I wanted it to.

'Well, she'll have her sisters to play with, won't she?'

I picked up the piece of yellow chalk she had just discarded.

'Well, she can still play with us, can't she?' I could see myself losing my friend from the capital.

'She won't want to – not now,' Sheila sniffed. 'You watch – she'll drop you now.'

I concentrated on my chalking. I had enjoyed the chats I used to have with Annie, usually in secret, in the Anderson shelter. She had had a tough life up to now. She told me hair-raising stories of how poor they were in Silver Town, how she saw rats running about around the houses there and the children had to play on little more than rubbish tips. The house they had was very old and dirty and she had to sleep in the same room as her brother, George, and sister, Helen.

I had listened with politeness, never telling her that I, too, had recently been sharing a room with John and Susan. She thought we were all very rich, having a nice big, new house, and I wasn't going to tell her otherwise. I was happy now that she had her family back with her and she could leave the Lannings. Mr and Mrs Lanning had been very kind to her, but their house was just not what Annie had been used to and she found it a great strain remembering to clean up after herself. There was no bathroom in their house in London, so the bathroom next door had been quite a plaything to Annie. She would play for hours with the water, turning the taps on and off and watching the steam curl round the windows. Mr Lanning told Dad about it over the fence.

'I wouldn't mind so much if it wasn't for the amount of coal I have to burn to keep that back boiler hot,' he said, 'and there's that little minx running it away down the plug.'

And Mrs Lanning had complained to Mum over the fence, 'She's not a bad girl, but I wish she wouldn't slide in her outdoor shoes all along my nice polished landing. You should see the scuff marks from her Blakeys, all along the lino.'

We walked home from school in silence. Sheila was sulking because I wanted to go, as usual, to meet Annie from school.

'She won't want you to,' she said. 'She'll want to rush home to see her precious sisters.'

So we made the journey, not talking until we reached the corner of our street. What a sight met our eyes! Everyone seemed to be out in the front of their houses and carrying things. Mrs Williams appeared with some blankets, Mrs Rolfe struggled through her gateway carrying a small white-painted table and there was my mum with some saucepans. Other neighbours were scurrying about with an odd assortment of household items and they all seemed to be heading for number 31. There at the door stood Annie's father, gratefully accepting the things and taking them inside. There was quite an air of excitement and everyone seemed to be chattering non-stop.

I caught Mum's eye.

'What's going on?' I asked.

'A man came round today from the council and asked if any of us could spare a few things for this new family. It seems they lost everything when the bomb dropped on them. They've got nothing at all left, so we are all giving what we can. I've just taken over some of the spare saucepans and an old kettle.'

'Poor things,' I said, staring across at the house.

Mrs Rolfe came puffing up to us. 'I didn't realise how heavy that little table was,' she laughed. 'Fair took it out of me carrying it over there. Still, I expect they'll find a use for it.' She brushed her hair back from her forehead. 'I was just thinking, Mrs Hathaway,' she said, 'what about those other people?'

'What other people?' Mum frowned.

'You know – those.' Mrs Rolfe jerked her head in the direction of the house on the bend – the house we were not supposed to talk about. 'They were bombed out, too. They can't have very much stuff in there, and there's quite a lot of them.' Mrs Rolfe spoke in a whisper.

'Yes, I suppose you're right,' said Mum. She looked round at all the activity. 'Shall we see what the others say?'

So with much whispering and gesticulating and much deliberation between the grown-ups more stuff was dug out of cupboards, sheds and attics and Mr Whitlock, who lived next door to *the house*, was elected spokesman. He picked his way up the front path, avoiding the bike wheels and cardboard boxes, the milk bottles and waste paper, and knocked on the door. I kept well behind the adults, watching progress from the safety of the far path. The door opened and there stood one of the women. She had peroxided hair, screwed up now in Dinkie curlers, a blouse fastened with two safety pins and a black skirt that was far too short for her, showing her knobbly knees and wrinkled, laddered stockings. She eyed Mr Whitlock with suspicion, listened to what he was saying, then craned her neck round him to look at the crowd gathered by the door. Then she smiled and waved the first person in. One by one the gifts were offered and accepted, the scruffy children running about in glee, carrying all they could. It was quite an evening, and we went in to tea at long last, tired and happy.

When at last I went to bed and said my prayers I felt that Jesus was listening this time because we had helped those poor Vackies. It was a lovely feeling. I didn't even mind that my hat was still lodged high up in that tree, and even less that Valerie had been so horrid.

CHAPTER 6

'I have to be very careful how I fill this in, so go away and find something to do.' Betty, sitting at the table with the ink bottle and Dad's blue pen, frowned at me. She didn't often tell anyone off, so I felt that this was something very important that she was writing.

'What is it?' I asked, kneeling up on a chair by her side and trying hard to look at the papers in front of her.

'They are joining-up papers,' she said, dipping the pen in the ink.

'Joining what up?'

'For joining up.'

She sighed, and bent her head over them. She had put her hair up into a French roll, which was all the fashion in those days, and I was fascinated by the black shininess of it. It was like a long dark sausage right round her head. When I said nothing she turned her head and looked at me, her lovely grey eyes kindly now.

'I'm going to join the WAAFs,' she said. 'That's the Women's Auxiliary Air Force.'

'You going to fly a plane?' I was aghast. 'Them planes get shot down!'

'No, silly, I'm going to be a driver.' She hesitated. 'Well, that's what I want to do.'

'But you'll have to go away,' I said.

'Yes, but everyone's joining up, and I think this is what I want to do.'

'What about your job?'

'Someone else can do that. There are lots of people to make hats, but not so many to drive lorries and things. Older people would like my job – some older lady who is too old to join up.'

This was exciting news. I had to tell Sheila.

'Betty's going to drive lorries for the air force,' I said proudly.

Sheila hitched up her knickers and eyed me with suspicion. 'Your Bet can't drive.'

'She can.' I rose quickly to my sister's defence. 'She must be able to or they wouldn't let her join up.'

'Bet she can't.'

We were sitting on the roof of the shed in Sheila's garden, and the tin roof was hot against the backs of our legs. I lifted my leg and rubbed it.

'This roof's too hot – let's go down by the stream.'

We dammed the water till it spread out to form quite a large pool and turned over stones to catch the little pale-coloured freshwater shrimps that lived underneath. Sheila's dress, tucked into the legs of her knickers, was wet and muddy. I watched her floundering about and thought that if my dress got in that state I'd be for it, but she didn't seem to get the same kind of chastisements that I did. It didn't seem fair to me. I longed to be as carefree as she. As I watched from my kneeling position on the bank, the tall grasses opposite parted and Anne Taylor and Joy Horwood from the private road round the corner from us came through. They stopped when they saw us. Sheila stopped and looked at them.

'What d'you want?' she asked, her hands on her hips.

'Nothing.'

'Take it and go, then. We're playing here.'

'Free country,' Anne Taylor, a pale little girl with pale eyes and paler hair, said.

'Clear off!' Sheila took a step towards them through the muddy water.

'No.' Joy Horwood lifted her head in defiance.

She was older than us by a couple of years or so, and I sensed trouble. I stood up.

'You'd better, or you'll be sorry.'

Sheila was in one of her fighting moods. She had been a bit that way since I told her about Betty, so I thought I would try to calm things down a little.

'We made this pool,' I said. 'We're catching shrimps.'

'And you're not helping us, neither.' Sheila was out of the water now and standing right up close to them.

'They can,' I said.

I had had a run-in before with Anne Taylor and she had got her sister Audrey to sort me out. My ears sang for hours afterwards.

'Clear off,' said Sheila again and stepped back into the pool, stooped low enough to scoop a handful of water and flung it at Joy.

She gasped and jumped back.

'You little brat!' she said, shaking her dress.

Another handful hit Anne on the legs and Joy was in the water, too, struggling with Sheila. I couldn't let my friend put up with that, so I went in, pulling and tugging to get Joy off her.

Anne joined in, and there was the most almighty fight between the four of us. We kicked and punched each other, pulling each other's hair and trying to push one another over. First Anne went over, disappearing beneath the water and coming up gasping and spitting. Then over went Sheila and I, having been pushed simultaneously by Joy, but as we went over we pulled her with us and the fight finished, as fast as it had begun. We all dragged ourselves out on to the bank, coughing and spluttering, soaked through and silent. Without another word we went off in different directions, wondering what all the anger had been about. I was wet right through to my knickers and vest and wondered how I could explain the state I was in. I had made up my mind to blame it on to some Vackie kids. I would say I'd never seen them before and that they pushed me in. But when I got indoors no one took any notice of me, so I went upstairs and changed, putting my wet stuff under my bed.

Downstairs, in the kitchen, Mum was getting Pat ready for bed. She sat in the sink while Mum washed her hair, her fat pink body shiny with water and her head a white cap of soap. Betty was leaning on the draining board, her chin in her hands, watching, and they were deep in conversation.

'Where do you reckon they'll send you?' Mum asked.

'Don't know, but I'm really excited about this, Mum. Joyce Fillis is going too, so we may be able to stay together.'

'Can you drive a lorry?' I asked, collecting some of the suds in the palm of my hand.

''Course not, silly,' said Betty. 'They will teach me how when I get there.'

'Get where?'

'I don't know yet.'

I thought it was all a bit pie-in-the-sky – couldn't drive, didn't know where she was going! I didn't think much of this joining-up lark.

Mum lifted Pat out of the sink and sat on the chair, wrapping her in a towel.

'Go and find John,' she said to me. 'It's time you were all indoors.' She glanced at me, looked away, glanced again. 'What are you doing in that dress? Where's your green one?'

'I didn't like it, so I changed.'

'What have you been up to? You're telling me fibs, I think.'

She scrubbed away at Pat's hair, fighting to keep her on her lap.

'Go on – find your brother,' she said, and I sped off, glad not to have to pursue that line of conversation.

Next day, when we came home from Sunday school, Mum was in the kitchen, frowning, and on the table was my wet green dress, my knickers and my vest. She was not amused.

I nursed my sore legs, lying on my bed, and wondered if Sheila had been told off.

I convinced myself that she had, although, knowing past happenings, I began to doubt it. Why didn't her mum seem to care how dirty she got? It was a very unfair world.

The day arrived when Betty would leave, and we all trooped down to Wingfield Hospital, which was the bus terminus, to see her off. She had Dad's big suitcase and Mum's little leather holdall, and she looked very smart in her new grey coat and little hat. I wondered what she would look like in a uniform.

She promised to write to us all as soon as she was settled in, and the bus trundled off up the road, leaving our silent little group on the pavement.

'She'll be all right,' said Dad, taking Mum's arm.

I pushed the pram behind them.

'She's very young, Ted,' said Mum.

'She's nineteen,' said Dad. 'I was fifteen when I went.'

'Gosh,' said John, 'fifteen!'

'Yes, fifteen. I put my age on – told them I was sixteen. You had to be sixteen, you see,' said Dad. 'I wanted to go, because all my friends had gone.'

I wondered why anyone would want to go and fight in a war. It seemed silly to me. Betty had a lovely job making ladies' hats in a big shop in the town and she had all of us to come home to every night. She could go to the pictures with Joyce Fillis any time she wanted to because she was grown-up and she didn't have to go to bed early. I reckoned she was daft to want to go and drive great big smelly lorries.

Not long afterwards we had a letter. It was from Betty and she sounded very happy. I was pleased for Mum because she had been so worried about her. The letter cheered her up, and more so because it said that Betty would be at a place called Brize Norton. I had never heard of it – it could have been in Timbuktu for all I knew, but apparently it was only a little way away from us so she would be able to get home quite often.

I felt very proud of my WAAF sister and boasted about her to all who would listen.

'Is your Kathleen going?' I asked Sheila. Kathleen was her oldest sister.

'Might.' Sheila kicked at a stone, aiming it at the opposite kerb.

'Bet she doesn't,' I said spitefully.

'Bet she does, then,' Sheila pouted, 'and I bet our Brenda will, too.'

That was something that I hadn't bargained for. Perhaps both her big sisters would, and that would mean that only one of mine had made the Big Move. I began to look at Lila in a new light, watching carefully for signs of any forms she might just happen to be filling in. But no, the weeks and the months passed and still Lila cycled off every day to work. I was just happy that there was no sign of either Kathleen or Brenda going, because that gave me one-upmanship in the street.

Most of the kids' fathers had gone by now, and many of their mothers were working at the factory, making ammunition and petrol cans and the like. Well, they said they were making ammunition, but Dad told me that the factory made aeroplane parts and tanks and things. I suppose the ammo story was *their* bit of one-upmanship.

It was lovely to get a letter from Betty every so often, and we would all crowd round while Mum read it aloud. She had learnt to drive and was driving ambulances on the aerodrome. With one letter was a photograph of her in uniform and we all ooed and aahed over it. She looked very grown-up in her cap. Mum carefully put it in a frame and stood it on the mantelpiece, and I could tell from her face that she was as proud as Punch of her eldest daughter. Once or twice I caught Dad having a look at it, too.

One day I came home from the park to see a lorry outside our house, so hurried along to see what was going on. As I opened the back door I could hear laughter and chattering. Who could it be?

I slowly opened the door into the living room and there, as smart as a carrot in her blue battledress jacket and trousers, was Betty. She held her arms out to me and I ran into them. I couldn't speak because of the lump in my throat.

'Hello, you,' she said, hugging me. 'Been a good girl?'

I nodded. The jacket felt strangely rough against my cheek.

It was then I noticed, sitting in the armchair, another girl in the same uniform. She was smiling over her teacup.

'Hello,' she said, and her voice sounded funny.

'This is my friend,' said Betty. She turned to the girl. 'And this is Nan.'

'Why does she talk funny?' I asked.

Mum jumped in quickly: 'Don't be rude. Say hello nicely.'

'Och, that's OK. It's my Scottish accent, I think,' the girl said, placing her empty cup on the table. 'That was a lovely cup of tea, Mrs Hathaway.'

John came rushing in at that moment, as eager as I had been to see who was there. When he saw Betty he rushed at her, then, seeing the friend, stopped dead.

'That your lorry?' he asked. 'Did you drive it?'

Betty laughed. 'Yes, we had to take it for repairs and we're on our way back.' She looked at the clock. 'We'd better be going. We're slightly off route, and by golly we'll get it if we're found out. Couldn't come so close to home without calling in, though. Tell Dad and the others that I'm sorry I couldn't wait, but I'll get a weekend pass soon so I'll see them then.' She picked up her cap from the arm of the chair and put it on.

We all went out to see her drive away. I felt strangely tearful, but Mum was excited and red-faced with pride.

That was the first of many visits from both men and women from Brize Norton. Betty had evidently told them that if they were passing there would always be a cup of tea and a chunk of Mum's home-made cake. We had never had so many visitors before, and we kids would listen to all the different accents – Scots, Welsh, Irish and the lovely sing-song tones of Norfolk and Suffolk. There were exciting events like damaged planes trying to make landings and ambulance crews rushing out to take off the injured. I tried to imagine my gentle Betty being witness to such awful scenes.

Then came the day that Lila decided she would like to join the WRNS, so we went through the form filling and all the usual things, like 'All the Nice Girls Love a Sailor' and 'The Fleet's in Port Again', until eventually there we all were seeing her on to the bus with her cases. The house began to feel empty and we missed the evening chat and arguments that used to go on between them. There was plenty of room round the table at mealtimes now, but it was lonely and strange.

The house was soon to come alive again though, and I couldn't wait to go to school the next day to tell Sheila that Grandma Ward and Grampy were coming to live with us because of the bombing in Croydon. I was hopping about on her doorstep long before normal school time.

'You're early,' said Mrs Williams, opening the door. 'She won't be long.' And she closed it again.

It was cold and I hugged my scarf round my chin, wishing Sheila would hurry up. When she at last appeared, eating a slice of toast, I grabbed her arm.

'Why are they staying with you?' she asked, scrunching away.

'I told you – because of the bombing.'

'Are they bombed out, like the Vackies?'

I didn't like the idea of my grandparents being grouped together with those poor wretches that had arrived homeless on our doorstep. I hesitated, thinking how I could make it sound better.

'They're bombed out, I think, but they're not poor. They still have got clothes and furniture and stuff.'

We waited for a small convoy of army lorries to pass and then crossed the road. Sheila pushed her blue hands into her coat pockets, and I was glad that Betty had knitted my nice warm mittens.

'I don't think I'd like my gran living with me,' Sheila sniffed. 'It'd be like having two mums to tell me off all the time.'

'My Gran and Gramp are very nice.' I was quick to defend, although I didn't really know much about them, having only seen them on fleeting visits at Christmas when they had stayed with Auntie Enid and Uncle Sid.

And arrive they did. Joan and I were put into Betty's room in her big double bed so that they could have the large room for a bedsitter. Dad fixed up a curtain rail and hung heavy dark-green curtains across to separate their living end from their sleeping end. With the double bed, wardrobe and chest of drawers it was very cosy behind those curtains. The other end of the room had an armchair on each side of the fireplace, where Dad had lit a beautiful fire and placed a coal bucket and a pair of tongs. There was a table with a vase of grasses and two dining chairs. Under the back window stood a bookcase full of books that I couldn't wait to look at. I assumed that Gran and Grampy had brought all this stuff with them, but it must have come while I was at school because I cannot recall to this day seeing it arrive. The whole effect was comfortable and utilitarian and Gran soon made it more like home by covering the walls with framed photographs and pictures of flowers in vases. One or two handmade samplers hung by the fire, and I thought I had never seen a warmer or cosier room.

My idea of Gran being like the kindly old lady in fairy stories was soon dispelled. She was always on to us to help Mum.

'You're not going out to play till you've helped wash up,'

she would say, her snow-white neatly set hair trembling and her earrings flashing. She didn't wear long swingy ones like Gran Hathaway, but neat little studs, nestling in the pink fleshiness of her earlobes.

'Tut-tut, look at the state of your knees – off you go and scrub them. I don't know how your poor mother puts up with you' and 'Alice, isn't it time these children were in bed?'

I thought of my dear mum as a child being constantly badgered with lots of *You mustn't*s and 'Do this' and 'Do that', and yet she loved her mother so much. I would take to going the longest way home if I knew Mum was out shopping or something rather than have to tidy my room or lay the table under the stern eye of Gran. It was not that I minded either of those jobs, but you can bet that I wouldn't do them to Gran's standards and would have to do them again and again until they passed her inspection.

Mum would just glance over what I had done and say, 'Lovely, thank you.'

Grampy was different again. He was a charming man and a special favourite with us all. He joked with us and taught us humorous little rhymes and songs, and we would go into fits of laughter over his various ways of dealing with the Germans.

One I remember especially well was the 'club' method. Grampy said that we should send out party invitations to all the German Army, then when they arrived at half past three on a Sunday afternoon, all dressed up and expecting jellies and cake, we would open the door to them, saying, 'Oh, do come in.' And as they came skipping through the door, Grampy, behind the door with a big club, would bonk them one by one on the head.

He would demonstrate this by standing behind the living-room door armed with a walking stick and saying, 'Come on in, nice Germans, deedle-deedle-dee' (that was supposed to be the partygoers tripping in through the doorway) 'BONK!' And he would bring down the walking-stick handle on imaginary heads. 'Gotcha.' Then he would stride in, walking stick behind his back, a look of sheer innocence on his face, and say, 'Goodness, look at this – a whole conked-out German Army. We'd better tell the War Ministry that the war's over.'

Every evening he would insist on we three youngest going into their room and sitting at his feet, by the fire, while he told us stories about London and Croydon Airport and when Mum was a little girl. Then he would ask us about our day. Usually it would end when Pat, who was two by now, fell asleep and Gran would carry her along to bed. If we stayed too long, and she was still awake, Gran, who was usually sewing or crocheting in the opposite chair, would tap her hand on the arm of the chair, catch Grampy's eye, and glance knowingly at the clock on the mantelpiece. If he chose not to notice she would cough or tut. We got to know the signals and went off reluctantly to our beds.

One such evening, drowsy in the flickering firelight, I passed a photograph back to Grampy. It was of Mum when she was about seventeen, sitting in the light of a fire, looking at a book, and Grampy had been telling us about it. As he took it he noticed on my hand a wart. It was an ugly thing which Mum had been trying to get rid of for a long time. She had tried everything she could, but still the thing grew. In fact it was such a horrid thing that no one at school would hold my hand in country dancing and I was very conscious of it. Perhaps that is why he had not noticed it before – because I was always trying to hide it. Well, he noticed it now, and studied it for a long time, his moustache working as he concentrated.

At last he said, 'I think we can do without that, don't you?'

'It won't go, Grampy,' I said.

'It will when I've worked my magic. You mark my words, my girl: by Christmas you won't even know you ever had it.'

I told Sheila of this wonderful news.

She scoffed. 'He won't get rid of it,' she said, 'not unless he burns it off. My mum had a friend with warts all over and the Doctor put her in an oven thing and scorched them all off.'

I was horrified. Was he going to put me in the oven?

'But he said he'd magic it away,' I said, biting the fingers of my gloves, pulling a stitch and watching it form into a hole.

I stared at the pink end of my finger in horror as I remembered they were Joan's gloves that I had sneaked out because I had left mine at school.

'He ain't got no magic, dafty,' said Sheila. 'He'll burn it off – you'll see if he don't.'

I asked Annie about warts and she said they had to be cut off, so I wasn't very happy when we went to say goodnight to Gran and Grampy that night. I tried to keep my hands out of sight in the folds of my nightie and was pleased to be wearing one of Lila's cast-offs, which was voluminous on me and offered lots of hiding places. Grampy caught my eye, gestured for me to sit on his footstool and reached a small bottle down from the shelf. It was dark in colour, ribbed, with a cork in the top. I looked at it with great apprehension as he pulled the cork out. Sue wrinkled her nose and moved closer to Gran.

'Pooh, it stinks,' she said.

It did.

'Magic potions always smell funny,' said Grampy. 'Powerful stuff this – and very magical.'

He waved the bottle under his nose and smiled up at the ceiling. He took hold of my hand and laid it flat on the grey flannel of his knee.

'Keep it there,' he said in a strange voice – rather like a vicar.

He tipped the liquid on to the cork and gently wiped it over my wart. It was icy-cold – so cold I gasped.

'Go away, horrid thing,' he whispered. 'Go away and leave Nan's hand. She doesn't want you' and 'Begone from this small white hand.' We children sat enthralled at this strange behaviour, firmly believing he had magic powers, so it was a shock when he suddenly recorked the bottle and said, quite normally, 'OK, that's it for now. That's it for tonight. I think we've scared it. Now it won't hang about long.'

I stared at my cold hand. It smelt funny, but still the wart was there.

'Oh, it won't go as quickly as that,' said Grampy. 'It's a grand old fellow and it's going to take a bit of shifting. We'll have another go tomorrow.'

'Are you really magic, Gramps?' asked Susan, her eyes wide.

'Of course – all Grampys are.' He replaced the bottle on the shelf. 'Now, off to bed or your mother will be after me.'

As we went along the landing I heard Gran say, 'Really! You shouldn't fill their heads with such nonsense. What if that thing doesn't go? You'll have some explaining to do.'

'It will go.' I could hear Grampy stoking the fire with another log. 'You mark my words.'

The cork rubbing continued for some time and it became a night-time ritual. At first everyone was interested to see the progress, but still the thing sat there, refusing to go, and after a while they lost interest, although I still sat with Grampy while he stroked and talked. I had faith in him if no one else had.

Then one day Annie, with whom I was playing marbles in the gutter, said, 'Look at your wart!'

I looked. I stared. I couldn't believe what I was seeing. It was all soft and pink, not hard, scratchy and grey. I fled, leaving even my best alley-gob in the dirt, and burst into the kitchen where Mum was sitting talking to Gran.

'Where's Grampy?' I cried.

'What on earth's happened?' Mum jumped to her feet. My wild eyes must have frightened her.

'Where is he?' I almost shouted.

'Calm down, child,' said Gran. 'What's happened?'

'My wart! My wart! Where is Grampy?'

'He's gone to the gyppos to get some logs,' said Mum. 'He'll be back shortly.'

But I couldn't wait. I was off. As I sped past Annie I didn't even notice that she was putting my marbles into her little cotton bag. She pulled the drawstring up tightly when she saw me and I hesitated for a split second before racing off again, not sure of what I had seen.

'What's up? Where you going?' she shouted after me.

'To find my Grampy,' I bellowed back.

I didn't hear her reply. My only thought was to find my magic Grampy.

The Gypsies lived in a collection of caravans out beside the main road that ran past the end of our street, and they sold firewood and bought scrap iron, although they hadn't much scrap iron lying around these days – it had all been taken for the war effort.

I ran into the yard before I realised that there were dogs. They seemed to be everywhere.

'Don't run, kid,' shouted a tall, dark man with a battered hat on his head. 'If you do, they'll 'ave ye.' He bellowed at the dogs and they dropped to the ground with their ears down.

He came towards me, kicking out at one of the dogs. 'Bloody curs,' he said. 'What d'ye want, girlie?'

'My Grampy,' I said, looking round the yard in desperation. 'He came to get logs.'

'Over there.'

The man pointed with a bony brown hand, and there was Grampy, deep in conversation with an old woman in a long black coat and a shawl. His little log cart was piled high with logs, so I knew he wouldn't be long in coming, but I couldn't wait. I walked over to him, longing to run but aware of the dogs watching.

'Grampy,' I said, and he turned to look at me.

'Oh, hello, dear,' he said. Then, to the lady: 'This is my granddaughter – well, one of them anyway. This is Nan.' He smiled at me, placing a hand on my shoulder. 'Anne, I should say.'

It was not very often that I was called by my proper name except by teachers and the Doctor, and it sounded strange. I felt I was in a dream in this strange place, with strange people. Mum would never let us go near the gyppos, let alone in their yard. I felt that today was different, though. Grampy's magic was working, and here I was in the very place I had been told not to enter.

Some days seemed very different from others for peculiar reasons, and even now I get that same feeling, almost as if I am not really doing what I am doing, giving a dreamlike quality to everyday things.

The old lady smiled at me, showing exceptionally white teeth, and held out a brown hand. I thought the brown might be dirt, so I hesitated to give her mine, but she took hold of it anyway and studied me closely.

The tiger-like smile didn't falter as she said, 'You have a sweet face, but beware of being taken for granted because of it. You have a strong aura.'

I thought she meant that I smelled, so I drew back.

'There is a long, long road ahead of you, but you will tread it with strength and reach any goal that you want to.'

She leant even closer and her breath was brackish. She looked at my hands, holding them both and studying first the backs then the palms. I didn't mind this now that the wart was fading away. It wasn't nearly so noticeable.

'Pretty hands to take on the world,' she said. 'You will be a musician – no, an artist, more likely. You can play the pinano.'

I guessed that she meant the piano, so I shook my head. 'No.'

'We left our piano in Croydon,' said Grampy sadly. 'Pity. You could have learnt to play – your mother can, you know.'

I didn't know. In fact I was very surprised. Mum had never said that she could.

'Come on,' said Grampy at last, taking hold of the handles of the cart. 'Help me push.'

He tipped his hat to the lady and we trundled the logs across the potholed ground towards the gate. I had been so taken by the Gypsies that I almost forgot what I had come for.

'Look, Grampy,' I said, pushing my hand under his nose. 'It's going.'

He smiled. 'What did I tell you?' he said. 'Faith and magic – works every time.'

It was a very happy little girl that went to bed that night.

I was going to go along a long road, playing the piano and painting wonderful pictures with wart-less hands.

'Get your coat on, Nan. I've got a surprise for you,' said Mum one Saturday morning. 'Joan, give an eye to the little ones, and keep an eye out for John. He's off playing somewhere. We won't be long. I just want to take Nan somewhere.'

I pushed my arms into my coat sleeves.

'Where are we going?'

'Not far. I think you'll be pleasantly surprised,' said Mum.

I hurried along beside her and we turned the corner at the end of the road. We seemed to be going to Auntie Enid's.

'Are we going to Auntie's?'

'No. Wait and see.'

Mum was smiling, and she stepped out at quite a pace, causing me to have to take a quick little run every so often. We went into Auntie Enid's road, but turned off into a side road, where Mum was studying the house numbers intently. At last she opened a gate and started up the path of number 42. She knocked at the door.

'Who lives here?' I enquired in a whisper.

At that moment the door opened and a fair-haired lady appeared. She smiled at Mum.

'Mrs Hathaway?'

'Yes. Is she here?'

'Come in,' said the lady, and we stepped into the hallway of her house.

The middle door opened and a girl of my own age stood facing us. She was a sturdily built girl with black hair in a thick plait down her back, and dark eyes. She looked me up and down and gave a timid smile.

'This is your Cousin Barda,' said Mum. 'Say hello.'

I think I muttered something like 'Hello', but I stared at this new cousin. The last time Cousin Barda had been to see us we were too young for school, and now here stood this eight-year-old girl. But what was she doing with this stranger?

'Barda is here because of the bombs,' said Mum.

At this she flung herself at Mum, hugging her tightly and crying. Her tears fell and her shoulders heaved.

'Oh, Auntie, let me come and live with you. I don't like it here. Please, please.'

Mum patted her back. 'Oh, darling, I wish you could, but we don't have a lot of room now, with Gran and Gramp there, too. You'll be fine here with this nice lady and you're only round the corner, so you'll be able to spend lots of time with us. You can come to tea any time you like and play with Nan and Sue, and when we go for walks or to the pictures you can come, too!'

I felt a lump in my throat and leant forward, laying my hand on the shuddering back.

''Course you can,' I said.

The lady stood by, her head on one side, watching.

'She doesn't seem at all happy,' she said, 'although I'm sure we've done our best to make her welcome.' She patted her hair into place. 'I'm sure I don't know what to do.'

With more promises of a welcome at our place and trips out, Barda's sobs subsided and we left her, red-eyed and bowed, on the doorstep. In silence we walked home again, and it wasn't until we reached our gate that Mum spoke.

'Poor little soul,' she said. 'I wonder if it was a good idea to visit so soon. She's only just arrived and must be feeling very much on her own. It was lucky that we managed to find her somewhere so close to us, but I didn't realise that she wouldn't understand that we were trying to do our best.'

'Why can't she stay with us?' I asked. 'There would be room if we put another bed in with Joan and me.'

'I doubt if we'd squeeze one in – would we?' There was a look on Mum's face that meant an idea was forming. 'I do hate to see her so unhappy. We'll see what your father says.' And she marched indoors.

I told Sheila about my cousin and was surprised that she was not as enamoured with the fact as I was.

'I bet she's stuck-up, like your Gran and Gramp,' she said sullenly.

'She's not.' I pictured the crying Barda. 'She's OK.'

We told Annie and she said, 'Is she a Vackie?'

I hadn't thought of her as one, but had to admit that if she had come down here because of the bombs then she must indeed be one. Somehow the thought that a cousin of mine could be like one of those poor wretches that had arrived without homes, without clothes, without furniture and looking so sad, was something I didn't want to accept.

'No,' I said.

'Yes, she is,' said Sheila.

'She's all right, then,' said Annie, and linked arms with me, smiling with a great sense of satisfaction. 'When is she coming to play with us?'

Although Barda played with us and was lucky enough not to have to go to The Poplars with Annie, but was found a place in our school, I found it difficult at times to mediate between her and others in our gang.

She spoke beautifully and had impeccable manners, which made Sheila nudge me and whisper, 'She is stuck-up!' as often as she could. I was torn between my friendship with the kids from the street and Barda, and tried desperately hard to stay loyal to both. We saw a great deal of her because, apart from sleeping at the house in Benson Road, she spent nearly all her time at our place, eating with us and going shopping with Mum.

Then one day I found her breaking her heart in the Anderson shelter. She was huddled on the bench furthest from the door, and I could just make out her shape in the gloom. I approached her with trepidation because I was sure that one of my friends had upset her. I waited for her to turn on me, but instead she just cried and wouldn't speak. I went for Mum. It seemed that she couldn't face going back to Benson Road and wanted to live with us, so that night she was squeezed into the double bed with Joan and me, and Dad was dispatched to tell Mrs Shelock in Benson Road that she was staying with us. I was overjoyed, and it was very late when the three of us got to sleep. She was the happiest girl in the world.

All through the summer holidays we played. We roamed the length and breadth of the golf links, jumping the stream and climbing the trees. We caught grasshoppers in the dell and little dark-brown lizards that lurked beneath stones in the damp grass. The only sign of the war was the occasional air raid, but that, too, was a game to us, wrapped in blankets in the Anderson shelter.

Barda was an intelligent girl and told me a lot of things about flowers, birds and trees. She was the youngest of the three daughters of Auntie Dolly and Uncle Fred, who was Mum's brother, and they lived in Wimbledon. She had been going to a private school, and they had to wear uniforms and straw hats and things.

I thought it very grand to have such a cousin. She must have thought the way we lived so very different. They even had a telephone.

I, of course, related all this to Sheila, and immediately knew that I had made a grave mistake.

'Told you she was stuck-up,' she said. 'Well, you can have her. Annie and I will play on our own.'

And they did. I didn't see them all through the long, hot weeks, but I had Barda and we had lots to keep us happy. There was a new girl in the flats – Joy Hillier – and we made friends with her because she had a little dog and it was fun to take him with us on our jaunts. She didn't mind Barda's posh accent – in fact, they became very close, and I felt I was being pushed out, so I began to pester Dad about a dog. Why couldn't we have one?

Being close to Cowley Barracks, there were constant convoys of army vehicles up and down the main road, and we would sit on the wall of the flats watching them drive past. Some days there would also be long, winding columns of soldiers, too, and they would wave to us when the Sergeant wasn't looking. Sometimes we would fall in behind and march along as far as Wingfield Hospital, then pretend to be soldiers and march all the way back again. Being infantry regiments, their marching steps were very quick and quite suited to our little legs. It was great fun and filled many a day.

We were striding along one day when I heard John shouting my name, and I broke away to see what he was so excited about.

'Guess what?' he said breathlessly when I reached him.

'What?'

'We're going to have one of Judy's pups.'

'When?' I couldn't believe my ears – a dog!

'They'll be born next week sometime.' His eyes were shining.

'Who said?'

'Dad did! He just said that he'd had a word with Len's dad and we could have one.'

And so we did. He was black and tan and we called him Paddy. When we brought him home on the first day, Mum looked at him and said, 'Very nice.' And then she looked at Dad and her eyes said, 'Another mouth to feed, another to clean up after.'

That was not all. Shortly after the arrival of Paddy, Auntie Dolly and Barda's sister, Sheila, moved in, too. Again there was a big shift round and Susan and Pat were moved into Mum and Dad's room, and Auntie Dolly and Sheila went into their room. They had the sitting room downstairs as a living room so that they could have a bit of privacy, but all ate with us, in relays. We kids thought it such fun having so many people in the house, but I expect it drove my poor mum to distraction.

I remember her saying to the lady in the Co-op one day when asked how she coped with it all, 'But they are all family.' That was our lovely mum – anyone in trouble and she was there.

Of course, Barda was delighted to have her mum and her sister with her, and Gran was happy to have her family gathering under one roof.

She said, 'Well, there's only Deezie to come and then we're all here, with Enid just round the corner.'

'Oh, no, Mother,' said Mum, 'you've forgotten Mabel and Nellie.'

'Oh, do you think we could all squeeze up a bit more?' laughed Gran.

'Heaven forbid,' said Mum.

Actually, I found out later that Mabel had gone to live with Nellie in Wales, taking all the family with her, so they wouldn't be coming – not to stay. But at Christmas they all came and Auntie Enid had to open up her house to them, although she herself had two Vackie boys living there. What a Christmas that was!

CHAPTER 7

Christmases were especially hard during the war because of the rationing, and Mum had been storing up all she could for weeks ahead. The weekend ration cards that Betty and Lila had brought when they came on leave had been used for all the extras, like dried fruit, tins of meat, tinned fruit and condensed milk. With these Mum managed to make Christmas puddings and cakes and mince pies. The birds were no trouble – Dad just went down to the chicken run and wrung a few necks. Saucepans and baking dishes were swapped about between neighbours because most of them had been given up when we had the salvage men round collecting for the war effort. Metal was very precious and every scrap that could be spared had gone. Even the front gates and railings from our houses and the parks had been cut down and carted away. This didn't deter the women in the street. They were going to have Christmas at all costs, and they scurried about from house to house, borrowing the receptacles necessary to prepare a feast.

With Gran and Grampy, Mum, Dad, Auntie Dolly, Uncle Fred (who was on leave from the navy), Sheila, Barda, Auntie Deezie, Auntie Mabel, Auntie Nellie, Mabel's daughter Janet, Lila (who was also on leave), Auntie Enid and Uncle Sid, Joan, John, Sue, Pat and me, we had a wonderful Christmas. There was not much in the way of presents – mostly home-made things like pinafores, socks, hankies, gloves for the children, cheap bottles of Woolworth's scent for the ladies and Woodbines for the men (loose and wrapped in newspaper) – but what a time we had! We ate till we were bursting, lit the candles on the tree and sang carols. Grampy told us a ghost story and Gran sang her own Christmas song.

Then it was charades. Auntie Enid, who had always wanted to go on the stage, organised this, so, apart from just the miming bits, we had to dress up, too. This caused arguments and squabbles and lots of laughter, until Joan, getting into the mood for acting, showed off a little too much, leapfrogged over Dad, who was bending down to retrieve Pat from under the table, caught her foot and fell heavily. She sustained a broken collarbone, which broke up the festivities somewhat. However, undaunted, we decided to carry on the party on Boxing Day.

Right in the middle of 'squeak, piggy, squeak' the siren sounded and there was a hasty retreat to the Anderson shelter. Twenty people and a dog in an Anderson shelter made for ten is quite a squash, feet, legs and arms all over the place, but the laughter continued and every so often we would hear one of the aunties say ''Blige me?' which seemed to be a favourite expression of these London ladies. This, in turn, caused laughter and I'm sure the Germans, had they landed and walked up our garden path at that moment, would have wondered what was going on. Here we were, in the middle of the war, with an air raid in full swing, and these crazy people were enjoying Christmas. We sang, recited poetry and played guessing games in the dark, because Dad had forgotten the matches for the candles, and then we heard someone outside. Stealthy footsteps were coming down the ladder outside the door. He shushed for silence, and we held our breath. The footsteps stopped.

'What is it?' whispered Auntie Deezie, somewhere in the dark.

'Shh!' Dad said.

'Oh, lor!' – Mum.

'Who's there?' – Auntie Enid.

'Be quiet!' – Gran.

Someone was fumbling with the latch on the door. There was a deathly hush inside now – not even a sound of breathing.

The door slowly opened.

Paddy barked and was immediately silenced.

'Everyone all right in here?'

It was only Harold, in his waterproofs and a tin hat shiny with rain. With great gusty sighs of relief we assured him that we were and he tossed Dad a box of matches to light the candles. Then he went off to air-raid-warden somewhere else. When the all-clear finally sounded we clattered up the ladder to continue our festivities indoors and drink a toast to 'absent friends' and 'the King'.

All in all, apart from Joan's arm held high on its frame and coated in plaster of Paris, and the disruption of the raid, it had been a glorious Christmas.

With the holiday behind us it was back to school, where I was astonished to find that Barda had been put up a class with the older children because she was too brainy for our level. I still had Joy, but wanted to remake my friendship with Sheila, who didn't seem very anxious to reciprocate.

'Want to play skipping?' I asked her in the playground, watching Barda laughing and joking with a group of bigger girls. 'I've got my rope.'

I produced the length of hairy string from my pocket. Sheila looked at it with disdain.

'Maureen Bye's got a real one with red wood handles. I'll play with her,' she said.

I leant against the rough brick wall surrounding the lavatories and felt thoroughly miserable. Even Joy's attempts to entice me into a game of tig did nothing to lift my spirits.

At home again, waiting for my turn to have tea, I listened intently to something Joan was telling Mum: 'It would be good if we could join, Mum,' she was saying. 'They teach us to make things to sell for the troops.'

'When is it?' asked Auntie Dolly, cutting bread as if her very life depended on it.

'Every Wednesday night at half past six till half past seven, and Mrs Everett said she would walk home with us after because of the blackout.'

I glanced at the black curtains drawn across the windows to stop German planes seeing any lights from our house. Why on earth would Mrs Everett walk anyone home because of our curtains?

'Well, I don't mind as long as she does,' said Mum, plonking the jar of home-made jam on to the table. 'What's it called again?'

'King's Messengers,' said Joan.

'Funny name,' said Cousin Sheila, daintily cutting her bread into little squares.

'It's something to do with God or Jesus,' explained Joan. "That's why it's at the church.' She scowled at Sheila. 'Silly.'

'How did you hear about it?' asked Gran.

'Father Beddoes told us at Sunday school.' She turned to me: 'Didn't he, Nan?'

I nodded. I couldn't remember him saying anything, but thought I had better give the impression that I took notice of everything he said at Sunday school. I had probably been too busy trying to find naughty bits in my Bible, or gazing at the pointed nails, hammers, ladders and thorns on the rafters above the altar. There were so many things to take your attention in the church, and Father Beddoes was not the most interesting of men. However, the idea, of going out on Wednesday evenings and making things for the soldiers began to appeal to me. What sort of things did soldiers need? Guns? Tanks? Planes?

'Could I go, too?' I asked.

'I don't see why not,' said Mum, and so Joan and I became King's Messengers.

We gathered in the hall of the church, the altar bit having been hidden behind the sliding panels that were drawn across to make a large, empty hall. The chairs, normally in neat rows for the congregation, were all pushed back against the walls, four deep all round, except for about a dozen which were placed round four large trestle tables right in the middle. Here we sat making, not tanks or planes, but painted cocoa tins with a hole in the lid for string, oven gloves, cushion covers, painted tins for spills or tapers, pincushions and aprons. Mrs Everett, one of the church helpers, chatted away to us, telling us that everything we made would be put up for sale to buy wool so that the women members of the King's Messengers could knit scarves, gloves, pullovers and balaclava helmets for soldiers, sailors and airmen. Most of the materials we used were purloined from home and collected up in big cardboard boxes, from which we all picked what we needed.

When we had been going for a few weeks we were presented with a little gilt badge to wear – a little gold crown with the initials 'K.M.' on it. I was very proud of this and wore it with dignity. I felt that I belonged to Jesus's special club.

Mrs Everett kept her word about taking us all home afterwards, and we were glad of it, because there were no street lights and no lights showing from the houses. It was illegal to show any kind of light, and when there was heavy cloud it was indeed very dark.

One evening, walking us to our house, having deposited all the other children at theirs, she began to talk of another idea. Father Beddoes had had the thought of opening the little hut behind the church after evensong on Sundays as a place for the soldiers to gather to play records on the old gramophone, play cards, darts and things like that. How would we, she asked, like to help prepare sandwiches ready for them after the evening service? Of course, we would be gone home before they all arrived, but she could do with some willing helpers beforehand. We jumped at the idea even though it would mean having to go to evensong as well as Sunday school.

So it was that Joan and I put on our aprons every Sunday at seven and made sandwiches and brewed tea in the little kitchen at the side of the church hall. The ladies made rock cakes and buns and we piled them on to plates and carried them across the cinder yard to the hut, laying them out on long tables, and putting up the little green-baize card tables on their spindly legs, making sure that the blackout curtains were drawn, and that there were plenty of logs stacked by the old black stove. Our perk came in the shape of a stolen bun, tucked up our knicker leg to be eaten later. The buns were never as good as Mum's, but stolen fruit is always better, and we would eat them, stuffing them into our mouths and giggling, usually in the cloakroom or the boiler house. One day I took some cheese home to Mum and got a whacking for my troubles.

We enjoyed our little efforts to help. King's Messengers and the sandwich making were my contribution to the war effort, along with the usual paper collecting and holding skeins of wool while Auntie Dolly or Gran wound the wool into balls to cast on yet another blue, navy or khaki pullover or start endless scarves. The clicking of needles and the clacking of the women round the fire in the evenings became a way of life. Yards of knitting collected in boxes awaited collection by various organisations. Needles were guarded jealously, and if a knob came off it was quickly replaced with a blob of sealing wax so that the stitches wouldn't come off the end.

Mum was never very good at knitting, but her time was equally busy making skirts and coats for us, turning unpicked garments and re-sewing them into anything we might need. She could make a beautifully tailored suit for Joan or a coat for me or Susan out of discarded coats of Gran's or one of the aunties. Although clothes were also bought only with clothing coupons, we always looked well turned out and people would remark on our appearance when we were out walking. Of course this didn't apply to playing clothes, and sometimes I think we must have looked very odd in our assortment of garments garnered from various first and second cousins, who all seemed to be older than us. My favourite things were a pair of pea-green woollen slacks, shortened to fit, so that they resembled bell-bottoms, and puckered round the waist with a brown leather belt that had once been Dad's. I knew that it was Dad's because when he went to put it on one day he found that the length had been halved and holes made along its shiny body.

He held it up to us all congregated round the fire, and said, 'Who's the culprit?'

No one owned up – indeed they couldn't, because I had been the one with the leather knife from the shed and a skewer.

'Right, come on,' he said. 'Let's see who it fits now,' and one by one we had to stand in front of him while he tried it for size.

There were so many holes in it that it fitted everyone except the adults, but I knew that he suspected me because as he fastened the buckle on me he winked.

When everyone had had a go he frowned and said that he couldn't be sure, but he thought it was someone who needed it to keep up their trousers, and as it would look rather nice on pea-green ones he would give it to me. And he did. So, without the walloping I thought I would get, I became the true owner of the belt; and although the boys in the street offered me everything they could think of for it, I kept it for as long as the trousers held out. If I remember correctly, I think I still managed a swap with someone for something, somewhere.

* * * * *

There was always an air of excitement when we had a letter to say that Lila or Betty was coming home on leave. Mum would be in the kitchen making sure the food would go round and glad to think that they would bring extra ration cards with them. There was great activity around the house as we fitted up camp beds and made sofas into beds to accommodate them if they managed to both get home at the same time – which wasn't very often, fortunately.

'What time will they be here?' we asked Mum a thousand times a day.

'Sometime on Friday' came the vague reply.

'Can we go and see if they're on the next bus?'

'You'll wait up there all day. Could be any time.'

'I don't mind.'

'You'd do better to stay and help Auntie, or Grandma, or something.'

With fits of the fidgets and lots of rushing to the window, we would get into such a state of excitement that eventually we were allowed to go to the top of the road and sit on the flats' wall to watch for the buses. When one of them did get off the bus there was a mad rush to help with cases and carry handbags, and we'd provide a royal escort to the front door. Then back we would go to await the second arrival, repeating the performance all over again.

Then would come the unpacking: hands and arms all over the place handing out coat hangers, rushing up to bedrooms with anything that we could manage, and all the time knowing that somewhere within the depths of the case would be little treats for us. Lila was an officer's steward and would bring us tins of salted peanuts, which brought squeals of delight because they were something that it was impossible to buy locally. Betty would have bars of dark chocolate and strips of liquorice and sometimes even sherbet dabs, which we would devour with great relish.

When the initial clamour had settled we would gather round and listen to their tales, and they would say how lovely it was to be home, sitting round the fire, listening to the radio, laughing and relaxed. Mum and Dad were always so happy when they were home that I would go off into the dell or round to Sheila's house when it came time for them to go back as I couldn't bear to see the pain in their eyes. Even Dad would brush away tears as he waved them off, and that was something that I could never bear to see. I had seen Mum's tears several times, when we were listening to sad stories on the wireless or when Mrs Currill's mother had died, and when the lady from the paper shop told her about someone's baby dying – but to see Dad tearful, that was another thing.

Sheila's mother knew when it was time for them to go because I hadn't been round for a few days and then, suddenly, there I was again.

'Bet and Lila going, then?' she would say.

It was nice to have Sheila back as my friend. She had become used to having Barda around and had come to a sort of compromise with me. There was a new Vackie girl living with the two elderly ladies in one of the flats near Joy. We felt quite sorry for her because she had been taken in by two frumpy but kindly sisters – at least 100 years old, we thought. She was nine – the same as we were at the time – and she had to always wear a woollen hat and a thick knitted scarf folded across her chest and pinned with an enormous safety pin at the back. It was so thick that poor Eileen had to walk with her arms held away from her body, giving the appearance of a badly stuffed doll. Her stockings were woolly, too, and a deep ginger colour, and on top of these she wore hand-knitted ankle socks.

'In case I catch cold,' she would explain mournfully.

That wasn't all. One day, as we were playing on the golf links, making sandcastles in the bunkers, and searching for anything that moved in the stream, Sheila said, 'I wanna wee,' and disappeared into some bushes, closely followed by Barda. I stood throwing stones into the water, awaiting their return, and Eileen stood by me with a pained expression.

'What's up?' I asked.

'I wanna go, too,' she said.

'It's all right – no one can see you in there.' I pointed to the bushes. 'Go on – we'll wait for you.'

'Can't,' she said, crossing her legs.

''Course you can.'

'No, I can't.'

Sheila emerged, pulling up her drawers.

'What's up?' she asked.

'She wants to go,' I said.

'Go on, then.' Sheila, adjusting her skirt and petticoat, gestured towards the tangle of blackberry bushes. 'It's OK. We always go there, don't we, Nan?'

I nodded, watching Barda's head appear over the top of them.

'I can't though, cos of my coms,' wailed Eileen, moving from one foot to the other, 'and I'm bustin'.'

'Your what?' asked Sheila.

'Coms.'

'What's them?'

Eileen lifted her coat, then her skirt, then her thick white flannel petticoat. We all stared in amazement, for underneath was the weirdest garment we had ever seen. There made out of coarse cream-coloured wool with tight-fitting legs almost to her knees, were the coms.

'Golly,' said Barda.

'Cripes,' said Sheila.

'Cor,' I said.

'What funny knickers!' breathed Barda.

'They're not knickers. They're coms,' said Eileen quietly.

She lifted her clothes even higher and we stared as the full extent of the garment was revealed. It went all the way up to make a vest as well. We were intrigued.

'How do you get into them?' asked Sheila.

'Buttons, here on the front,' said Eileen.

'They're awful,' I said unkindly.

'How do you go to the lavvy?' asked Sheila.

We were so interested in the design of the things that after a lot of arguing poor Eileen found herself gradually undressing to show us them in all their horrific glory. She stood there looking absolutely ridiculous, her clothes in a heap by her feet, while we walked round and round her in awe. With the trapdoor at the rear dissolving us into fits of laughter, Eileen decided she had had enough. She was now shivering with cold and the tears streamed down her face. Notwithstanding the fact that the poor kid was positively bursting to answer nature's call, and that she looked a picture of abject misery, we, her so-called friends, rolled about on the grass, roaring our heads off. I really believed I had never seen anything so funny.

Eileen fought with the flannel petticoat, which was inside out, wiping away her tears with her hands.

'You're awful,' she sobbed. 'I can't help it. They make me wear 'em. They say they'll keep me warm.' She tugged at the armholes angrily, turning it this way and that in an effort to get it the right way up.

Barda, lying on her back, her knees up, resting on her elbows in the grass, said, 'Now you're undressed, why don't you have a wee?'

Eileen cast her a withering look and continued to struggle into the petticoat. She picked up the dress and shook it.

'Shan't,' she said.

'Can't,' laughed Sheila.

'Leave me alone!' shouted Eileen.

'Temper, temper!' said Sheila.

At long last, with all her clothes on again and her face stained with tears, we all set off for home. Eileen walked quickly ahead of us, while we brought up the rear, dissolving into quiet giggles every so often. We didn't see her in her grey tweed coat, red woolly hat, grey scarf, red gloves and thick stockings. All we could picture was her skinny figure in those off-white combinations. She threw us knife-like glances over her shoulder, striding with great determination through all the rough grass and swampy ground until we reached the top of the dell opposite the flats. Here we stopped.

'What're we gonna do now?' asked Sheila.

'I could go and call for Annie and play by the shelters.' I suggested.

Eileen leant against the lamp post, her chin on her chest, swinging one leg.

'Coming?' asked Barda.

She shrugged her shoulders. 'Don't mind,' she said.

'You'd better go and have a wee first,' said Sheila.

'Don't matter now – I've peed meself,' said Eileen.

CHAPTER 8

I was playing with Paddy in the garden when Joan came out through the kitchen door.

'We've got to take some wool to school tomorrow,' she said.

'What for?' I asked.

'Knitting.' She sat on the log horse, scuffing the sawdust into little piles with her hand.

'Knitting what?' I asked.

Paddy had lost interest and ran off towards the henhouse.

'A bag for our cups,' said Joan.

We had all been asked to bring a cup to school because at playtimes we now had to line up in the hall and have a hot drink. The weather was now getting bitterly cold, and as coke and coal were in short supply the powers that be decided that a warm drink would be beneficial to us; so we were to have either warm milk or a milk drink, such as Horlicks or Ovaltine. Mum had supplied us with a mug each for this purpose.

'We'd better ask Mum for some wool, I suppose,' I said.

'She says we haven't got any – only the wool for the army stuff, and we can't use any of that.'

I decided to hold a conference with Annie, Sheila and Barda about this as no doubt they would have to find some, too. We gathered in Sheila's dad's shed.

'We ain't got none,' said Annie.

'Nor us,' said Sheila.

The Williamses had recently taken in some lodgers – evacuees from London, Mr and Mrs Tanner – so Sheila's one-upmanship in the street was definitely good.

'I'll ask Mrs Tanner,' she said. 'She does knitting.'

And she fled.

We knew by her face as she returned that the answer was negative.

'No, she says that all the wool she uses is from things that she unpicks.'

'Where on earth can we get some?' asked Barda.

We didn't know the answer so we played I spy for a while, then went our different ways to see what was for tea.

On the way to school next day we discovered that most of the other kids were experiencing the same problem.

'My mum says that if they want us to knit bags then they should give us the wool,' said Margaret Smith.

'My mum says that you need coupons for wool and she can't spare none,' said little Shirley Bye.

'Mrs Tanner unpicks things to get wool,' said Sheila.

In bed that night I thought over what they had all said. My eyes came to rest on my school jumper hanging over the end of the bed. That was wool. Then they settled on Joan's cardigan on the chair. That was wool, too.

In the morning I sat eating my breakfast. Auntie had a lovely pale-green jumper on; Mum had a pale-blue one, all wool; little Pat, in her high chair, quietly stuffing porridge into her mouth, wore a pink knitted dress. Wool. I was becoming obsessed with the idea of knitting a bag. Everywhere I looked that morning there was wool, and yet none of us kids could get hold of any.

In the bathroom, on the side of the bath, was Dad's brown pullover. I felt its texture. Yes, it was definitely knitted. I carried it out into the kitchen, where everyone seemed to be talking at once.

Above the babble of voices, I asked, 'Mum, does Dad want this?' and held it aloft.

At the same time John was asking if he could go to Paul Forrest's house after school for tea.

'No, I don't think so,' said Mum.

That was good enough for me. I folded up the pullover and picked up my coat.

'I'm off to school,' I called, and went to call for Sheila.

'Look what I've got.' I held out the garment and watched her eyes widen.

'Miss will be able to unpick it for us, won't she?' I asked.

'Yeah, 'course she will,' said Sheila.

But Miss couldn't.

'This is not hand-knitted,' she said.

'It's wool,' I said.

'Yes, it's wool, but it was made on a machine and can't be unpicked,' she said.

'Mrs Tanner unpicks things,' I said, my heart sinking.

'Not like this, dear,' said Miss.

'I wanted it for my bag,' I said.

Miss Cordon smiled kindly. 'That's all right,' she said, 'I've managed to get hold of some for the knitting class. You take this home to your mother and tell her it wasn't suitable, and don't forget to thank her.'

We were all given a small ball of bright-blue wool and some thick wooden needles and shown how to cast on. The pullover hung in disgrace over the back of my chair.

'It wasn't any good,' I said to Mum when I got home.

'What wasn't?' she asked, throwing the big tablecloth over the table.

'This.' I held up Dad's woolly.

'For what?'

'Unpicking.'

'Goodness, child, what are you talking about?'

Mum dealt plates like a card player.

I explained what Miss had said, and Mum stopped in mid-throw and stared at me.

'But I didn't say you could have that,' she said.

'You did – you said, "I don't think so,"' I said.

'I'm sure I didn't. That's Dad's best pullover.' She took it from me and frowned. 'Honestly, Nan, sometimes I wonder about you. You imagine all sorts of things.'

'I don't. I asked and you said it would be all right.'

Gran appeared at that moment and I knew that she had heard every word.

'Don't tell lies, Nan,' she said. 'I don't think for one moment that your mother would say that you could have a perfectly good piece of clothing. Clothes cost a lot of money.'

'She did,' I protested.

'Don't say "she",' said Gran sternly.

I scowled.

'And don't scowl. You ought to know by now that your mum and dad don't have much money, and with all your mouths to feed and clothes to put on your backs it is very hard for them.'

She picked up a piece of bread from the cutting board and put it in her mouth.

'Mum has to feed you, too,' I said.

Gran's mouth dropped open. Mum turned from her slicing.

'Nan,' she said.

'I'm sure I don't know what to make of this one,' said Gran, her cheeks pink.

'Well, she does, and you eat a lot,' I said.

'Nan, go to your bedroom,' said Mum, 'and don't come down till I call you.'

I did as I was bid, turning at the door. 'You could give Mum lots of money if you wanted to. Grampy said that you had a piano, and they cost lots and lots of money.' I opened the door. 'You're rich.'

'GO!' Mum pointed with the bread knife.

I went.

I took the hiding from Dad later and had no tea. Joan came to bed with Barda and they told me that Gran had grumbled about me all evening. They undressed and got into bed, Joan's cold feet making me pull away sharply.

Barda's voice from her little bed at the foot of ours said, 'They are rich, though.'

'Are they?' asked Joan.

'I've been to their house, and though ours is big theirs is bigger.' She huffed and puffed as she drew her legs up into the warmth of her nightie.

'I knew it,' I said quietly.

'But they aren't rich now,' said Joan. 'They've had their house bombed.'

There was silence for a few moments, then Barda said, 'No, it's not been bombed, only a bit damaged. I heard my mum telling Grampy that when she went to see what happened there were all bits of wood over the damaged windows and the roof of the conservatory and that all the stuff had been taken away and put into storage until they come back.'

'Well, I'm jolly glad about that,' said Joan. 'I thought that the bombs had flattened it all.'

'I wish we were rich,' I said.

'They're very unlucky, though,' said Joan, a drowsy voice now, from under the blankets. 'We have at least got our home.'

I had to agree on that point, but my tummy was beginning to rumble and I thought wistfully of the tea I had missed.

Next day as we crossed Rock Edge, carefully crunching the thin ice on the puddles, I asked Barda about her home. It was strange, but I had never been very curious about where she lived or what her home was like. Now I was eager to find out.

'There's Mum and Dad; Freda's away in the WAAFs, like your Betty, and there's Sheila and me. You know what school I used to go to. Our house is very nice – quite big really – with lots of lovely trees and things like that. Even the street has trees down each side.'

I tried to imagine our street with trees. It would look quite nice, I supposed, but there wasn't really room. The road was narrow enough and the paths took up quite a lot of space.

'Have you got friends and things in the street like I have?' I asked, stamping on a shard of ice so that it splintered into a million crystals.

'No, all my friends are at school.'

'Who do you play with at home, then?'

'We aren't allowed out to play. We do things at home after school, then at weekends I usually go up to the stables and help with the horses. Sometimes, if I work well, I'm allowed to ride them from the yard to the paddock.'

'What's a paddock?' Sheila, who was trailing behind us, called.

'A field,' said Barda. 'Surely you know what a paddock is?'

Sheila shrugged and kicked at a frosty tuft of grass. 'Oh, yeah,' she said. ''Course.'

We turned into St Anne's Road, which led to the school. I had decided that all other questions would wait until Barda and I got home after school. I didn't want any antagonism between the two of them, and I felt that Barda's way of life was so different from ours that Sheila would get angry again and call her a snob, to cover her own shortcomings.

Jimmy Skivington was coming towards us. He was well known as a bit of a bully and was usually avoided by us. If he was in the vicinity we would walk all round Headington, past Bury Knowle Park, down Wharton Road and back through Margaret Road and St Anne's to get home. By this time he would be gone – the coast would be clear. Going to school was easier because he was either too early for us to meet along the way or he would be really late, skulking into assembly, hoping no teacher's eagle eyes would spot him, and once again the smaller and younger children had escaped a bashing.

Well, there seemed no such luck today, for there he was, his hands pushed well down into his jacket pockets, his shoulders hunched, his head forward, his jaw jutting and his piercing blue eyes relentlessly fixed on us.

'Oh, no,' said Sheila, 'it's Jimmy Skivington.'

'Crikey,' I said.

'There's three of us,' said Barda strongly.

He was a tall boy, or so he seemed to us, with untidy hair; and although his clothes were not particularly poor, he always looked scruffy because he would not tuck his shirt in and the buttons on his coat were never all done up or all undone, just fastened here and there.

'Watcha, kids,' he said, and smiled at us. Smiled! 'No point in going to school. No coke. Boiler's off.' And he walked on straight past us.

We breathed sighs of relief. Several other children were running towards us now, laughing and shouting.

'Hooray!' they shouted. 'No school. We've got no coke!'

That was good enough for us, and we, too, made for home.

Coal and coke were very scarce at this time and if we went to the cinema Mum always insisted that we wore extra woollies, scarves and gloves because there was never any heat on. At home we were lucky because with the Gypsies just around the corner there was a constant supply of logs for the fire, Grampy stacking and carrying two or three times a week to ensure we didn't run out. I had been in other kids' houses where they had no fire at all, and the place was bitterly cold. Dad said it was up to everyone to do their best with what they could get, but I know that he had given a helping hand to many in the street.

Mr Rolfe worked for Butterfield's Butchery and many an evening we would hear whispered voices at the front door, and next day we would have sausages for breakfast. One of us would be told to carry a bag full of vegetables or a dozen eggs along to his house. We didn't realise at the time that there was quite a lot of bartering going on. Tim Jones's stepdad, Mr Thomas, wasn't above a bit of poaching and we would occasionally have rabbit stew after a surreptitious visit from him. Off he would trudge with eggs or something in exchange.

The same happened with little jobs in houses where the man of the house was away in the forces. Dad would disappear with a screwdriver or a bag of nails and a hammer, doing little repair jobs for the family. People would bring garments to Mum to let down hems as the kids grew out of them and turn collars on school shirts as they wore out, because clothes were very hard to get hold of once the month's coupons had gone. The whole street became a little community of its own with everyone looking to each other for help, comfort and guidance, and we children grew together more like a village than a town street, almost like one family.

We were still not allowed to have much to do with the Vackies in the corner house, though. The littlest one, Dawn, appeared one day with her hair shaved off and great splodges of purple stuff dotted all over her naked head. Mum went almost berserk when she saw it.

'Impetigo,' she almost shrieked. 'I don't want to see any of you over there.'

John was mystified. 'What's inthetigers?'

'Nasty horrid scabs.' Mum shuddered. 'Ugh!'

'Does it make your hair fall out?' I asked.

'No, the Doctor cuts all your hair off.'

'Why?'

'So that he can put that genital violet on,' said Mum.

Actually I had seen lots of the kids at school with gentian violet on their faces, but hadn't thought that it was anything that bad.

'Sheila had some last week,' I offered innocently.

'Oh, lor,' said Mum.

''Blige me,' said Gran.

'I think I'd like it better if you kept out of their house, then. I don't want anything like that here,' said Mum.

'Yes,' agreed Gran.

'Not go to Sheila's?' I asked in horror.

'Not if there's impetigo in the family.' Mum's voice was almost a whisper.

'But her mum's going out with Mrs Tanner tonight and we were going to sit with Arthur.'

Sometimes we were left to look after her younger brother while the Williamses and the Tanners went down to the corner house. Of course I had to get special permission for this, and we could only do it on a Friday night because there was no school the next day.

It seemed very grown-up being up so late, and we would pinch Brenda's lipstick and Kathleen's high-heeled shoes and pretend that we were Arthur's mum and auntie. The poor little chap was subjected to ear scrubbing and hair combing, shoved into his pyjamas long before he needed to be and bundled off to bed with stern warnings as to what would happen to him if he didn't go straight to sleep. We never carried out any of the violent threats, I am happy to say, but he must have been a very miserable little boy with us bossing him around. It was all a very good game for us, though, and as soon as he had gone up the stairs we would put the wireless on and dance to the music, tottering about in those ridiculous shoes and redoing our scarlet lips at regular intervals. We would even sometimes make a cup of tea – something that Mrs Williams always told us not to do.

'Don't you get touching the cooker, and keep the fireguard

round. Don't let that dratted cat in neither. He can come in when we get back.'

But, of course, as soon as they had disappeared down the road, Mogs would be let in to curl up on the sofa, and the kettle would be on. We always knew that at ten o'clock Mogs would have to be turfed out into the cold, protesting madly, the teapot emptied, cups washed up and put away, lipstick scrubbed off and Kathleen's shoes put back in the cupboard. We had it down to a fine art.

Wow! It seemed that all that was going to finish. I had been forbidden entry, and all because that Vackie kid walked down the street flaunting her shame.

Sheila wasn't too happy about it either.

'Your mum's a snob,' she said, scratching her head and scowling at me from under her frizzy fringe. 'What's wrong with my 'ouse?'

'I don't know,' I lied. 'She just said I wasn't to go into your house any more.'

'She's hoity-toity, that's what she is.'

'No, she isn't.'

'Clear off, then. I don't want you to come round anyway.'

She ran off, leaving me standing at the school gates, and I had to go home alone as Barda had found yet another new friend.

When I got home I went to meet Annie. She was pleased to see me because I hadn't been to meet her for a long time.

'Hiya!' she called when she saw me, and ran on her skinny legs as fast as she could, skidding on the frosty ground as she stopped.

We linked arms and laughed and chattered all the way home, past the Co-op and the barracks, making cheeky remarks to the soldier on the gates.

'What're you standing there for. Go and find some Germans to kill.'

'Cheeky young buggers,' he replied, sending us into fits of the giggles.

'Come over to my house after you've had your tea,' said Annie.

So I did. It was a very untidy house with tatty furniture and a kitchen that defied description. Her dad was sitting by the fire with a pullover on that was more holes than knitting, and no shoes on his feet, shoving his toes through the holes in his socks.

Her brother, George, was sitting on the torn brown lino cutting up newspapers into squares for the lavatory and Helen, her elder sister, who had just come in from work, was sitting at a junk-cluttered table eating soup. Mrs Whaley, her mum, who was fatter than when she had first arrived, dressed in an appallingly grubby overall, was endeavouring to find a place to sit amongst all the tumble of disorder.

They all made me welcome, though, and Mr Whaley said that I should get closer to the fire and ordered George to move back so that I could get in. Little Joannie, the youngest, had fallen asleep in the overstuffed armchair, but no one made a move to put her to bed.

Annie and I played with her doll, making clothes out of an old torn cot sheet until Mrs Whaley suddenly said, 'We ain't done yer 'air yet, Annie. Get the stuff.' And Annie went to the cupboard in the corner of the room and got a funny little comb and a sheet of newspaper. Then, as I sat watching, she knelt down in front of her mother and bent her head forward. With straight long strokes the comb was dragged through her hair, and every so often the newspaper, spread on Mrs Whaley's ample lap, was closely inspected. I watched, entranced. I had never seen anything quite like this before. At last the operation seemed to be at an end because Annie stood up, pushed her hair back into some semblance of order, stuck in a hairgrip or two and went over to the sofa. The sleepy Joannie was dragged unceremoniously over to her mother and, trembling and barely conscious, was made to kneel as Annie had done. Again the comb did its work, the rest of the family taking no notice whatsoever.

I was intrigued, but too shy to ask what was going on – I saved that for when I got home later.

'She was doing what?' My mum's face was a picture of horror.

I explained in detail.

'Don't you ever let me see you over there again!' Mum rubbed the towel furiously on Susan's wet hair. 'Go and get in the bath,' she said. 'The water's still warm.'

I bathed in the water left from Susan and Pat's baths, then draped in a damp towel went back into the living room. Mum was in the kitchen talking to Auntie Dolly. They talked in barely audible whispers, but I could hear what was being said.

'Nits' – Mum's voice.

''Blige me!' – Auntie Dolly.

'And our Nan over there. Gawd knows what she'll bring home here.'

'She needs a woodchip-and-vinegar wash right away.'

'Oh, lor.' Mum was very concerned about something.

I stood before the log fire, the warmth burning my legs, and the steam curling up from the soggy towel. What terrible thing had I done?

At last they came in.

'I don't want you to go to bed just yet, Nan,' said Mum. 'We have to wait for Dad to get in.'

She smiled at me, but I felt impending doom. Auntie fetched my nightie from the clothes horse and it was warm and comforting. I perched on the edge of the sofa. They sat opposite me, Auntie with her knitting and Mum with her darning. The clock ticked and the fire spat and fizzed. I watched the fidget, fidget of Auntie's needles and the weaving in and out of Mum's darning needle, one ear cocked for the sound of the side gate, which would herald Dad's arrival. I didn't think that I was in for a whacking because Mum had smiled, but there was something nasty in the air. I rocked back and forth, feeling the pricking of the coarse cloth of the sofa against my calves.

Was that the gate? No. I sighed.

Mum looked at the clock. 'Nearly nine,' she said.

A door upstairs opened and I heard the thump, thump, thump of Grampy's slippers along the landing. Mum reached up and turned on the wireless. Big Ben boomed out nine times. The door opened and Grampy came in. He smiled at Auntie and Mum, winked at me and pulled a chair up to the table on which the wireless lived. He leant forward, cupping his hand round his ear to hear better.

'This is the nine o'clock news,' said the man on the wireless.

The knitting needles clicked on; the darning continued. Grampy sat like a statue, listening to every word.

So this is what he did down here every night. I had often heard the nightly walk along the landing and in the distance the boom, boom of the big London clock. He came down to listen to the news. I tried to listen, but it seemed very boring. At intervals Grampy would turn to Auntie or Mum and smile, or frown or nod his white head. There were reports of things called troop movements and bombings and ships lost at sea. It all seemed dreadfully depressing to me. I looked at Auntie. She had stopped knitting and was listening intently to what was being said. It was something about submarines.

Suddenly her face lit up. 'That means Fred might be home again soon,' she said.

'Shh-h,' said Grampy.

When at last the news ended, the chatter started.

'They didn't say what sub,' said Grampy. 'Don't get your hopes up, dear.'

'I know they didn't, but it could be his. Home. Here in England again. Oh, I do hope so.' Her eyes were aglow as I'd never seen them before.

'All he said was that a submarine was in Portsmouth for damage repair,' said Mum.

'He didn't say Portsmouth. He didn't say anything about where it was,' said Grampy.

'Must be, though, musn't it?' said Mum.

Grampy shook his head. 'They never say where or what is going on. They can't – too many ears about.' He looked at me. 'How do we know that our Nan here isn't a spy?'

This was turning into a nightmare for me. 'First I'm told to wait for Dad to get home – heaven knows what for! – and now Grampy thinks I'm a spy.'

'I'm not, Grampy. Honest I'm not,' I said.

Everyone laughed and I realised that it was a joke. The fact that they laughed made me feel easier about Dad getting home. If I was in trouble there would be no laughing. The side gate clicked and thumped shut. I would soon know now.

Mum went out into the kitchen and I heard their voices, low and conspiratorial. Dad went out again into the shed. Five minutes later I was kneeling on a chair in the kitchen and the most awful pungent stuff was being poured over my head. Time and time again I suffered the obnoxious deluge, squirming and wriggling, but held firmly in place by Mum. At long last I was allowed to straighten up and a towel was wrapped round my head.

'Go in by the fire and give it a good rubbing,' said Mum.

I did so and knelt before the blaze smelling like a bag of chips from old Giles's shop.

'Best thing for nits,' said Auntie Dolly: 'wood chippings and vinegar.'

'What's nits?' I asked, peering at them through my matted tangle of hair.

'Fleas,' said Grampy. 'Go on – give it a good hard rub or it'll never dry.'

Mum knelt on the mat beside me and took over the drying.

'I don't want you to go in the Whaleys' house again, Nan,' she said quietly.

'Oh, Mum,' I wailed, 'she's my friend.'

'And she's not very clean. She's got nits.'

'How do you know?'

'That's what her mum was doing – combing out the eggs.'

I shuddered. 'What – in Annie's hair?'

'Yes.' She rubbed harder. 'This stuff will stop you getting them.'

I didn't mind the awful pong. I didn't mind the punishment my poor head was getting.

'Please get them out,' I pleaded.

So for a while I had to be content to play with the gang in the street. I couldn't go into Sheila's and I couldn't go into Annie's – the corner house was banned. This war thing was getting worse. Not only were people getting bombed out of their houses, Uncle Fred somewhere at sea, Lila and Betty away doing whatever they were doing, but now all the kids were getting inthetigers and nits!

The fact that I was playing with those same kids in the street seemed to go unnoticed by Mum, so it wasn't too bad, I supposed.

CHAPTER 9

The war dragged on. Newspapers were hidden from our innocent gaze, but we listened intently during mealtimes to all the news and heard of bombs and tanks and ships and planes. Occasionally there would be a slip of the tongue by one of the grown-ups and they would realise that not only had walls got ears but children had, too, and with a great deal of shushing and nodding of heads in our direction, eyebrow-raising and frowns, the conversation would be hurriedly turned around. We still did our little jobs in the evenings, tearing newspapers into squares for the hook in the lavatory, and spill making, while the grown-ups clicked and clacked at their knitting. Dad and Grampy pored over our school atlases, tracing patterns with their fingers and talking in low whispers. War was a great mystery to me, but very exciting.

John was intrigued by the movements of the troops from the barracks and would rush in to let us know when convoys were passing. He got a whacking for venturing as far as the marsh, where the guns were placed. There was great secrecy around that place, but somehow he had managed to get through and have a look. He made the great mistake of tearing home to tell Dad all about it, and received a leathering for his pains. In bed that night he told us girls that there were soldiers everywhere and these enormous guns with great long barrels pointing up at the sky. I didn't think it was very nice, but Joan, wiser and older, assured us that if any of those bloody Germans flew their planes over us they would get blasted right out of the sky. Barda agreed with her, so I guessed that it was all right.

We seemed to do all right as regards food. The two allotments were still producing and the hens were laying. We had reared a family of ducks, eaten all their eggs and then eaten them. Grampy Hathaway still thought that things must be pretty tough for us with our big houseful, because he would clomp up to see us at regular intervals, all the way from Morrell Avenue, some way away, carrying sacks of vegetables and baskets of fruit. We would hear him long before we could see him, because as soon as he caught sight of one of us he would give his own special whoop – a sort of 'Whoo-whoop' – which acted like a signal, and we would run to meet him.

For some unknown reason he called me Shirley, perhaps because as a baby I had a mop of golden curls and was likened to Shirley Temple. The golden hair had changed over the years to its dark brown, but he still said, 'Ho there, young Shirley,' whenever he saw me. He would present Mum with his sack of goodies, drink up the cup of thick dark cocoa she made for him, and set off home again. He was very like Dad to look at, but for his thick white thatch of hair, and we children loved him although he didn't say a lot. I can never recall ever having a conversation with him, just plenty of chatter from me and ahs and ohs from him.

Later in life I was told that he had eloped with Grandma Hathaway when she was a young girl. I wish I had had the courage to ask him all about it, but children were seen and not so much heard in those days, and it would have been such an impertinence to ask about such an indelicate thing. It seems that he had fallen for Rebecca (that was Gran's name), but she lived in The Quarry, a very close-knit community, and they didn't welcome outsiders. He was from Old Headington and was looked on with disdain by the Quarry folk. One day he just walked up and took her away, and no one even knew she had gone until some hours later. There must have been such an uproar, but they were married anyway and Gran never went back to The Quarry. Oh, when I think what stories he could have told me!

So, with all the home-grown produce and the livestock and Grampy, we always had plenty to eat, so the rations collected from the Co-op every Friday were well supplemented. Not so for many of the other families in the street.

Perhaps it was just that their mothers were not so adept at

making nothing do something, but when I was taking egg sandwiches to school for my playtime lunch, Sheila might have a slice of cold toast, sometimes without even a scrape of margarine. Whereas I had several skirts, albeit home-made remakes, she still wore faded cotton dresses far into the winter. And where my jumpers were warm but darned, her poor little skimpy outgrown woollens let the cold in through many holes. I walked to school with her on bitterly cold mornings when she was not even wearing a pair of socks and I felt guilty in my mended but warm black woolly stockings. Clothes were harder to come by than food in our house because the supply of clothing coupons had to cover everything from socks to sheets, so out would come Gran's little steel knitting needles and on four of them she would knit round and round and round until like magic a sock would appear. Worn-out cardigans would be unpicked and the wool skeined and washed, and several pairs of socks were born. Sheets were patched and turned, middles to centres, when they were paper-thin, then becoming pillowcases before gracing the duster box. Clothing coupons were used for shoes, wellingtons, John's school trousers and material for dressmaking. Give Mum a piece of material and her old Singer sewing machine and she would create stylish suits for herself, as well as dresses, skirts and blouses, shirts for the men, and nighties, pinafore dresses, aprons, coats and bonnets for the younger girls, and anything left over would be stitched round to make hankies. We would lie in bed listening to the whirr-whirr of the old machine and know that there would be something nice to wear in the morning. Coats and jackets were unpicked carefully with a razor blade, the material turned inside out and ironed. Out would come the fragile patterns and pincushion, and away she would go, recreating garments for us all.

Once when everything in the wardrobes had been made and remade and she was desperately looking round for stuff for winter clothing, a large box arrived from Auntie Mabel in London. It contained trousers, skirts, shirts and undies, all outgrown by our cousins and just perfect for us. It was like Christmas! Mum couldn't get over the fact that with all their problems, up there in London, with all that bombing and everything, they had taken the trouble to think of us.

''Blige me,' she said, wiping her eyes, 'if ever there was a Christian family,' and she delved deeper into the box.

Other little savers were going on all the time, but they became such a way of life that they were hardly noticed. There was a constant nag in the house to save water. Posters loomed everywhere telling us that five inches was enough depth to bath in. Practical Mum went one better: she would pile all three of us youngest ones in together, slosh us about like a lot of seals and whip us out quickly before the chill went off the water; then John would get in. After John, one more large enamel jug of hot water would go in followed by Joan. That was enough for one night, but the following night it would be Gran and Grampy, topped up for Auntie Dolly and finally our cousins, Sheila and Barda.

One evening Sheila had gone to something at her school and it was their bath night. In went Gran, in went Grampy, then Auntie Dolly with Barda. I don't think Barda was quite ready for this. She emerged, pink, warm and clean in her winceyette pyjamas, rushed through the hallway, caught hold of my arm as she ran past and dragged me into the cluster of coats that hung in the hall.

She pushed my head into the coarse tweedy overcoats, holding it there so I could scarcely breathe, then with her lips against the side of my head she whispered hoarsely, 'You should see! My mum's got titties. She lifts them up to wash underneath!'

We both dissolved into fits of laughter. The tears ran down our faces and our sides hurt. Mum peered out of the living room and asked what we were up to, but this just made us laugh all the more. And when Auntie Dolly finally emerged from the bathroom we couldn't contain ourselves. She stood there, holding her dressing gown tightly across her chest – the chest that was causing all the hysterics – smiled at us and swept past into the kitchen.

'I've weed myself,' said Barda, and we dissolved once more.

Betty, about this time, had met an airman and it was serious. She presented him to us one Saturday and he stayed for tea. He was very shy and spoke with a soft Norfolk tongue, which because of his awkwardness was very hard to understand.

He was very dark, with almost black eyes, and we girls giggled and nudged each other all through teatime. This undoubtedly made the poor chap even more nervous, but we didn't see it; and when he and Betty had at last gone back to camp, both Mum and Dad gave us a good tongue-lashing. In bed, Joan and I talked excitedly about Stan.

'Isn't he gorgeous?' breathed Joan. 'His lovely black hair.'

'Is he foreign?' I asked.

'No, 'course not. He comes from Norfolk. Mum said that he worked on a farm up there and he's only got one brother.'

'No sisters?' I asked.

'Only a brother. I wonder what he thought of us lot all staring at him?'

Barda's voice, muffled from under the blankets, said, 'Is Betty going to marry him, then?'

There was a long silence. Marriage hadn't entered our heads until then.

At last Joan said, 'I hope so – then we could be bridesmaids.' She turned over with a great sigh. 'Wouldn't that be lovely? I'm going to say my prayers now. Goodnight.'

The next time Stan and Betty came home Betty was wearing a very pretty engagement ring and Mum was getting flushed and excited about the forthcoming wedding. She rummaged in the cupboard under the stairs and brought out a bottle of Grandma Hathaway's plum wine and everyone had a glassful. Grandma and Grampy Ward and Auntie Dolly had two glasses each, which we children noted with a touch of annoyance as we were only allowed what Dad called a 'wetlips' from his glass. There was a lot of laughter that evening, and little whispered jokes between the grown-ups with a great deal of eyebrow raising and sideways eye movements. But all this was way above our childish minds, and all we knew was that soon there was going to be a wedding and that some of us, if not all, would be chosen as bridesmaids.

Almost at once Mum started making lists and juggling with food coupons, carefully stowing away dried fruit in jam jars and hoarding the dark-blue bags of sugar like little sacks of gold dust. Grandma Hathaway sent over several bottles of her home-made wines and Auntie Gladys, who was one of Dad's sisters, contributed some icing sugar which she had been saving for some unknown reason. Mum was very grateful for anything that would help because it had been decided that the reception would be at home and Mum, Grandma Ward and Auntie Dolly would do all the catering, There was a constant buzz of excitement and numerous lists were made, discarded and remade; recipe books were studied at great length, although many of them were totally out of the question because of the scarcity of ingredients.

The sewing machine came into its own and worked long into the night, turning out presentable outfits for everyone. Dad's grey suit was brought from the wardrobe, released from its prison of tissue paper and hung on the clothes line to rid it of the pungent smell of mothballs. Grampy Ward took out his best hat and held it over the steam of the kettle to reshape it and burnish the felt. Grandma Ward unpicked the flowers from hers and rearranged them round the brim, carefully stitching them into place again. I found all this very fascinating, and indeed picked up several tips which have all come in useful to me since. I held the patterns in place while Mum cut out; I learnt how to fill the bobbin on the machine for her; I watched and learnt how the best creases were put into trousers, ironed over a wet cloth and beaten with the back of a hairbrush. I thoroughly enjoyed helping Dad to get an almost patent-leather look on our shoes by spitting and polishing, and would sit in the shed with him having a good spit and not being told off for it. That, to me, was heaven itself.

Sheila and Annie were jealous. I knew it and yet I played up to it with everything I'd got. I enjoyed watching them squirm as I related all the activities going on indoors, and found the greatest pleasure in informing them that Susan and I were going to be the bridesmaids.

I preened myself all the way to school, and I shouted out to everyone on the way, 'Hello. I'm going to be a bridesmaid.'

After the register had been called I put up my hand and was given the privilege of informing everyone in the class of my news, glancing sideways to where Sheila sat.

'Our Kathleen's getting married,' said Sheila one morning as we sat on the wall by the flats waiting for Eileen Fowler.

'Liar,' I said.

'She is, then. She's going to marry Bert Tanner.'

'Not before our Betty,' I said.

Eileen came out at that moment, muffled up in an enormous scarf and knee socks over her brown woollen stockings. The curtains moved slightly and we knew that the two old ladies who looked after her were watching.

'They're watching us,' said Sheila. 'Nosy old buggers.'

'They like to know who I'm playing with, that's all,' said Eileen.

We set off up the road and Sheila turned round at the corner to stick out her tongue. The curtain jerked.

We made out way to Headington, intending to play in Bury Knowle Park, but it began to rain so we ran on to Rock Edge and sat beneath the overhanging rocky sides of the quarry.

'When's your Kathleen getting married?' I asked.

Sheila shrugged her shoulders. 'Dunno. I heard Mrs Tanner telling my mum that she'd had a letter from Bert, and he said so.'

Bert was in the air force and, obviously, visiting his mother and father at the Williamses' he had met Kathleen.

'Why isn't your Kathleen in the WAAFs or the WRNS like Betty and Lila?' I picked at the rough surface of the rocks. 'Or your Brenda for that matter.'

Sheila shrugged again. 'Cos they don't want to, I s'pose.'

'My cousin's in the ATS,' said Eileen, wiping her nose on her scarf.

We looked at her. 'What's them?'

'Army girls,' said Eileen.

'Oh.'

The rain stopped and we went on towards the park.

'I bet our Bet's wedding's better and posher than your Kath's,' I said.

'Bet it's not,' said Sheila.

The rest of the day was a constant bicker between us; and after all the embroidery that I had fed into the conversation about the wedding day, I hoped and prayed that it would be like a fairy tale.

At home things were gathering speed and dresses were hanging on hangers covered with sheets to keep them clean until the great day. Susan's bridesmaid's dress was completed and mine was taking shape. They were made in silk with a pretty pale-green all-over print of tiny flowers, short-skirted with puff sleeves and a frill over each shoulder from front waist to back waist. I loved the feel of the material and would sit running it between my fingers, enjoying its coolness. Every time the lid came off the machine I hoped that my dress would be worked on, but sometimes Mum was only turning sheets or patching pillowcases and I began to fear that if it weren't finished in time then Susan would be the one and only bridesmaid, and how Sheila would laugh! But it was eventually finished, and little headdresses of flowers made by Auntie Enid, white shoes and socks and silver horseshoes on a ribbon completed the outfits. Mum had enough material left over from our dresses to make one the same for Pat, but it was agreed that she was, at four, too young to be a bridesmaid. And, indeed, this was a wise decision because she could be quite a handful at times. Perhaps this was because Mum was always so busy with our bulging house that Pat was left a lot to her own devices and not watched quite as diligently as we had been during our tenderest young years. Coupled with this was the tendency for both Gran and Auntie Dolly to spoil her as she was the baby. Hence she was a rather difficult child, on occasions.

The date was fixed for 29 May and was to be at St Luke's Church in Cowley, and, of course, now we children were in a fever of excitement. I was in my seventh heaven – more so because our Betty's wedding would be before Sheila's Kathleen's, and I would be a bridesmaid before her. John was not at all excited, though. He seemed to think it all a soppy waste of everyone's time and energy.

Joan was being her important grown-up self, going through the service with us every night in bed, frightened that we might 'mess it all up' and 'spoil Bet's day'. I became very conscious of all this possibility that I might be the one to do so, so I listened intently to all she had to say – but there seemed so much to remember! It appalled me to think that at one stage Dad had to give our Betty away! How could he even think of doing something like that? Joan thumbed through her prayer book, reciting in monotones the strange words, and Barda and I lay and listened in awe. Perhaps weddings were not so nice as I had always imagined.

The tables (the big one from the living room and the little kitchen one) were put together and spread with a white sheet and simply covered with big plates of sandwiches, cakes and other delicacies, including Auntie Dolly's special sandwiches, with the crusts cut off (such dreadful extravagance), and Gran's little fancy cakes. Mum's sausage rolls (courtesy of Mr Rolfe and his association with Butterfield's) were piled up in the centre, and there were piles of plates and serviettes. In the vases at each end were cut flowers from Grampy Hathaway's allotment, and crowning the whole thing was a magnificent chocolate cake with one white gardenia (imitation) on the top. There hadn't been enough icing sugar by the time Mum had to make it, so she had to top it with chocolate butter icing, but it was truly sumptuous.

The weather was good, too, and by the time the car arrived for us most of the street were collected around our gate. I felt like royalty as I swept out and saw Annie with her mouth gaping at my appearance. I gave her a supercilious smile and climbed into the car.

I remembered everything Joan had told me and even managed to hold and return Betty's bouquet, which was vast and trailing, at the right times. And I didn't drop it once.

Back home again, I flirted outrageously with the best man – an airman called Dougie – and posed in the back garden for Grampy's Brownie, making sure I was well in the front each time. All in all it was a lovely day and Betty looked so beautiful in her lovely dress and veil that I didn't even notice that Dad had given her away.

CHAPTER 10

The air raids continued and the Anderson shelter was used most of the time. I say most of the time because we did become a little complacent about the raids, having only once been subjected to the noise of the guns from the marsh. Night after night Dad stood and watched the skies, but no enemy planes appeared on our horizons, only the long white spears of light from the searchlights, raking in vain across the night sky. So after a while we would huddle in the cupboard under the stairs again, where it was a lot warmer than the shelter. Indeed, there were times when we didn't even bother to do that, but stayed in the snuggly comfort of our beds, safe in the knowledge that, ever watchful, Dad would soon drag us out if danger threatened. The convoys of army vehicles became an everyday occurrence and we no longer ran and waved to them. The excitement came at the sight of the long lorries carrying wrecked planes.

'Cor, look at that!'

'That's a bit smashed up, ain't it?'

The twisted metal and broken perspex held a macabre fascination for us, little ghouls that we were, and we would beg, borrow or steal bikes so that we could follow the vehicles to the dump, about a mile away. Of course we were never allowed to get near the actual dumping ground, but would wait until the load had disappeared inside, then pedal back home to tell the kids that hadn't been able to get a bike that we had seen piles and piles of planes, both German and British – thousands and thousands of them.

We spent a great deal of time collecting newspapers and tying them into great squashy bundles ready for the salvage lorry that came round every so often. It would trundle slowly along and we would run up and hurl the bundles into the back, then as he reached the end of the street the driver would wave his arm out of the window and pick up speed into the next road. Jam jars were a source of revenue for us because if we took empty, clean ones back to the Co-op or the Home and Colonial Stores we could get a halfpenny each for them.

Joan had given up helping with the sandwiches for the soldiers, so I had introduced Sheila to it; but when she found out that she would have to come to church with me she dropped out. So I took Annie, who managed a couple of evensongs, filled herself with buns and sandwiches quite openly, spilled tea all over the place and then decided she had had enough, too. Joy was my next 'helper', but she, too, became disenchanted when Father Beddoes asked her if she wanted to come to confirmation classes with me when I started mine.

It was about this time that Auntie Dolly and Sheila decided that they wanted to go back to Wimbledon, and I was terrified that Barda would go, too. Mum was surprised when she found her in tears one day because she wanted to stay with us – but stay she did. She didn't seem at all worried that her mother and sister were going away, and I for one was glad that she chose to stay with us. We had become very close and I found her a good confidante. Huddled together in the dark confines of the Anderson shelter, we would whisper all our hopes and fears and visions of the future. We would dream up wonderful ideas and create a world where there were no wars or rationing or people going away from their loved ones. We swore that we would never lose touch with each other at the end of it all, when, we both knew, Barda would have to go back to her own home. I asked Dad one day while we were working on the allotment if she could stay forever with us, if he and Mum could make her one of their children so that she would be my sister, but he said that that was not possible and tried to explain that Auntie Dolly had been very upset that she had not gone home with them. Secretly, I passed this bit of information to Barda and she went very quiet. She said that she liked it better with all of us and hoped the war would last forever, so we both sat very quietly and wondered whether she had said something too dreadful. After a while she decided, and I agreed, that it was a wicked thing to say, so we decided to make amends. We would do a concert.

'We could get Auntie Enid to write us a play and make costumes,' I said.

'No. It's to be all our own work and we don't want any interference,' she said.

So night after night, as soon as tea was over, we would disappear upstairs and plan our show.

'I'll do my poem – "Old Meg She Was a Gypsy",' said Barda.

'I can sing something, I think,' I added.

'And perhaps we can both do a dance. I'll dress up as the man and you can be the lady.'

We scrounged a pair of redundant net curtains from Gran, and Grampy gave us one of his hats.

'But don't you get cutting it or anything. There's still a lot of wear in that.'

Lila's red silky scarf was dragged from the drawer and secreted upstairs along with one of Mum's petticoats that I was sure she didn't wear any more. In the airing cupboard was a lacy shawl that had been Pat's when she was tiny, and from the shed we took a pair of Mum's old high-heeled shoes that had really been thrown away. We set all these items out on the bed and looked at them.

'We can do lots with these,' said Barda slowly.

Personally I couldn't see what we could do, but I didn't say anything. I didn't want to believe that it was all a load of junk. Perhaps with imagination we could dress one of us as a lady, but that was about it. Even with Grampy's hat on her head Barda didn't look much like Fred Astaire.

'We need trousers,' I said.

Dad's and Grampy's would be too big and John was still wearing short ones, so where on earth could we get some long trousers?

Sheila, unknowingly, gave us the answer. She had been collecting rags for salvage and we met her at the end of the road with the big bundle slung across the saddle of Brenda's bike. My eyes fell immediately and greedily on it.

'Where've you been?' I asked casually.

'Getting rags.'

'Got much?'

'Yeh, loads. I've been all up the Slade and everyone's given me some.'

Barda and I walked with her towards her house.

'Where are you taking it?' asked Barda.

'Indoors. Then our Kathleen'll take it to salvage.'

'We can take it for you if you like,' said Barda. 'We've nothing else to do at the moment.'

'No, Mum says I've got to take it home first,' said Sheila. She wiped her nose on the back of her hand. 'Mum likes to see what I've got first.'

She pushed open the little home-made wooden gate that had replaced the iron one that had been taken away for scrap.

'See you,' she said, and trundled the bike through.

Barda and I stood and watched her negotiate the three steps down on to the front path.

Then: 'Come on,' said Barda, and set off at a run.

I panted behind.

'Where to?' I asked.

'Collecting,' she answered.

We worked our way all along Bulan Road and through Coverley Road, knocking on doors and asking politely for old rags and clothing, 'for salvage'.

Having nothing to carry it in, we soon resembled a couple of walking jumble sales, but amongst it all was just what we needed: a pair of black trousers. At home again, we dragged it all into the Anderson shelter to sort it out. Wonder of wonders, there was also a waistcoat! We hugged each other with joy.

The trousers and waistcoat joined the rest of our 'props' in the bedroom, and the concert was beginning to take shape. We decided that it would be two weeks hence on a Saturday, and that we would put a notice on the front gate to advertise it and charge a penny each to anyone who wanted to watch. This money would go to buy more wool for the forces. We felt good. Barda's statement about the war going on forever was eradicated.

'Where did all that rubbish come from, in the shelter?' asked Dad one day. 'There's piles of clothing down there.'

We had quite forgotten the rest of it.

Soon after that a letter arrived, and Mum read part of it to us. It was from Auntie Dolly and she was missing Barda so much that she wanted her to go home. I pleaded; Barda cried. Barda pleaded and I cried. But all to no avail, and the very next day we were waving her off at the station. She had gone. My world was empty. No one seemed to miss her at all and I thought how cruel the human race was. Sheila came round more often and Annie was always there, but it was Barda I missed so much. Bedtimes were the worst of all because Joan stayed up later now that she was working and it was lonely going to bed on my own. I would lie awake for a long time wondering if Barda was in bed.

She, too, would be finding it lonely, I thought. We used to say our prayers together, but there didn't seem any point in saying them out loud any more, so I would whisper them to myself under the blankets. I just hoped that God had good hearing.

Sheila said that she would do the concert with me, so we rehearsed all the dances and Sheila added her own interpretation of a tap dance to 'The Willy Woodpecker Song'. I tried to learn all of 'Old Meg', but could only manage two verses by the Friday night, so we thought that would have to do and hoped that nobody knew it all. The notice was crayoned on to a piece of cardboard and fastened to the gate with string. 'CONCERT TODAY,' it said, 'SONGS AND DANCES'. And underneath in smaller writing: 'ADMISSION 1d.' It wasn't till Joannie Whaley knocked at the door and asked what time it was that we realised we had forgotten to put that on, so I ran out with a pencil and wrote '2 o'clock' on the bottom. We had put a blanket over the clothes line to act as a curtain and would perform on the widest bit of the concrete path while the audience sat on the grass.

We were fixing the 'curtain' into place and making sure that it would draw when John appeared and stood watching us.

'I haven't got to pay a penny to watch, have I.' It was a statement, not a question.

'If you are coming to watch you will have to,' I said indignantly.

Sheila pulled the blanket across again.

'Yes,' she agreed.

'What – in my own garden?' he retorted.

'Yes.'

I dragged the blanket back again. It worked OK.

'Shan't come, then,' he said. 'Soppy anyway.'

'And you're not watching from the window,' I said, knowing his capacity for sneakiness.

'I'm going to the pictures. The Dead End Kids are on.' He kicked at our box of costumes. 'They're better than your silly concert.'

I looked at Sheila. She looked at me.

In the queue at the little Headington cinema, amongst all the pushing, unruly mob of kids we didn't give a thought to the others outside our gate, clutching their pennies and reading the hurriedly scribbled message, 'Concert Cancelled'.

The Dead End Kids were really good.

CHAPTER 11

I received my very first letter, delivered by the postman and addressed to me. 'Miss Anne Hathaway', it said, and my address was all beautifully written. I sat and stared at it. There was a twopenny-halfpenny stamp on it with the King's head and a postmark that said 'SW19'. I turned it over and over.

'Open it, then,' said Joan, a little irritated at the delay. She took another spoonful of porridge. 'Go on.'

Carefully I tore open the envelope. It was from Barda. She had remembered to write to me. She had started back at her old school and met up with all her old friends – well, most of them, because some of them were still away, evacuated. She had been up to the stables and started riding lessons. My heart began to sink as I read more and more of how wonderful everything was for her. She didn't say that she missed me or even asked how the concert was. She asked me to write back though, and that meant that she still wanted to keep in touch, as we had vowed in the musty interior of the Anderson shelter. She finished off by asking how Paddy was and if her tadpoles had turned into frogs yet, and if they had would I please let them go in the stream? It was a letter, but not quite what I had wanted to hear. I supposed that I would write to her – if and when I could find a spare moment.

I went to school that day glad that I had Sheila and Annie and Joy and all the other kids to play with. I had Paddy and I could catch newts and lizards and shrimps any time I wanted to. I didn't have to go to the stables to find animals; I could actually keep mine in jars and tanks, not have an hour's ride and then hand them back to their owners. I decided that Paddy and I were going to become very firm friends. He must have been a surprised little dog at all the attention I was soon giving him. I even dragged him with me down to the church for King's Messengers; but I was told that he couldn't come in, so I took him home again and gave up King's Messengers. If they didn't want my dog, then they didn't want me.

Joy had been given a puppy for her birthday and she called him Spiv. It seemed a funny name to me, but Dad said it was something to do with men who cheated with rationing and things, so I thought that it wasn't a very nice name to give a sweet little puppy. However, Joy and Spiv and me and Paddy went everywhere together. Annie desperately wanted a dog, but her mother had just had another baby so a dog would have to wait, and poor Sheila was scared stiff of anything that had hair (fur) or walked on four legs. It was as much as she could do to walk past her own cat – poor old Mogs.

If she saw us approaching with the dogs she would beat a hasty retreat behind the safety of her gate and say, airily, 'Oh, I can't come out – I've got to wash up,' or something similar.

Every day we found somewhere to go and something to do that included the dogs until one day they had the most horrendous fight. They flew at each other with snapping jaws and flailing feet. They made the most frightening noise I had ever heard.

I was in a state of panic, seeing Spiv on top of poor Paddy. I felt that I had to help him, so I waded in and tried to drag Joy's dog off. He snapped at my hands and wouldn't let go of Paddy. I screamed at Joy, who stood by with her hands over her ears. Spiv's head came round again and his teeth tore into my sock. I kicked at him with my free leg and he yelped and dropped my sock, and Paddy managed to wriggle free and race off down the road. Spiv took up the chase and Joy and I flew after them. An army lorry was coming down the road, and it screeched to a halt as the two dogs rushed headlong across in front of it.

'Keep your bloody dogs under control,' the red-faced driver bellowed at us. 'Next time I'll run over the buggers.'

The animals had safely reached the far side and disappeared at a fearsome pace into the distance.

Joy scowled at me. 'If my Spivvy doesn't come back you're in trouble,' she said.

She turned on her heel and went home, and I ran along behind her trying to convince her that he would, but she stalked on ahead and refused to talk to me. Of course, both of them returned later, but it was the end of our games with them, because Joy wouldn't come out to play and every time I saw her with Spiv after that she would grab hold of his collar and walk past. It meant that Sheila and Annie came back to me, though.

Lila was home on leave and Joan and I sat together on the wash horse in the garden, sharing the tin of roasted peanuts she had brought us. We closed our eyes as we munched, savouring every morsel, licking our lips for the salty taste and then feeling with forefinger and thumb in the tin for more. My greedy fingers picked up more than Joan thought they should and she tapped the back of my hand and frowned.

'Leave some for me,' she said.

I looked at her. The evening sun glinted on her pretty hair, worn now in a Veronica Lake style, hanging long and silky over her right eye. I also noticed that she had started to wear pink lipstick and peep-toed white sandals with a wedge heel. I wished I would hurry up and grow up so that I could emulate film stars. She swung her shapely legs, turned her face towards the setting sun, eyes closed, and chewed slowly on the nuts.

'All gone,' I said at last and got off the 'horse' to put the empty tin into the dustbin.

'Shall I tell you something?' said Joan.

I said yes, of course.

'I'm going in the Land Army,' she said, her eyes still closed.

'What for?' I asked.

'Because I want to.'

'What about your job?'

'But this is for the war – I'll be working on a farm to help out because so many of the men have had to join up and the farmers need everybody they can get to do the work.'

I couldn't imagine this film-star-like creature working on a farm. All that mud and cow-plonks! What about her nice white shoes?

'Where will you go?' I whispered.

'Don't know.' She shrugged, and a stray lock of hair moved on her shoulders.

I said nothing, just stared at her.

'The WLA,' she said slowly, as if it were magical.

'Does Dad know?' I ventured, glancing over my shoulder to the kitchen window.

'Yes, of course he does. He had to sign the papers for me. He thinks it's great. He says he's very proud of me.'

I had to admit that was probably true. He was proud of Betty and Lila, so why not Joan with her attempts to do her bit?

'And Mum, too?' I asked.

'Mum, too, although she did say I was a bit young.'

When at last she came home in that uniform – the breeches and socks and sturdy lace-ups, three-quarter-length coat and little round-brimmed hat – I thought how lovely she looked, and again the tears fell as we waved her off. She was not going too far away and promised to get home as often as she could. We had hilarious letters from her about all the mud and slush, but she seemed to be enjoying herself and had made a few friends. Then, unfortunately, she developed a dreadful rash all over her hands from the hand milking, and she had to come out. She went back to work at her old job at Mowbray's, where she sewed fine clothes for the church, beautiful robes and altar cloths, and in time the painful rashes disappeared. I liked her working there because she was allowed to bring home little off-cuts and I stitched them into little purses and mats for the top of our chest of drawers in the bedroom. It was nice to have her home again.

One bright summer's day John came hurtling in on his bike, threw it with a crash against the back wall and rushed into the kitchen.

'Guess what?' he shouted. 'There's Yanks in those buildings over the back of the Horses' Field!'

The far side of the dell was always known as the Horses' Field because it was home to a couple of old nags – we were not sure who owned them, because no one ever seemed to visit them, although they had a stable, and fresh straw and feed appeared at regular intervals. The stable made a fine place to play and the horses didn't seem to mind at all. Beyond this field there had been a lot of building activity going on for some time. We had no idea what was going up there, and so we took no notice – after all, there had been so much going on throughout the entire war, with shelters being built and sites used for scrap dumps where once there had been workshops and garages, so the sight of another crowd of workmen mixing cement and stacking bricks held no interest for us. Evidently this new development was a hospital, consisting mainly of Nissen huts, but with a few smarter brick-built constructions for administration. Yanks had been around Oxford for some time, but mainly in the city itself, so we didn't see very much of them unless we were taken into town by Mum for some shopping, which wasn't very often. They seemed to be so different from our soldiers. They were noisy and showed off a lot, chewing on their gum and whistling after all the girls. Mum, dragging us along with her from shop to shop as she looked for a bargain in shoes or some good cheap bed sheets, would tut and say 'Take no notice' in a hoarse whisper. This would only cause us to turn and stare at them even more and giggle to each other at their brashness. In the shops there would be more of them, leaning across the counters and chatting to the girl assistants until one of their supervisors would appear. The girl would scuttle off like a startled hare and the cheeky Yank would turn his attentions to the stern-faced manageress, who was no doubt flattered but held on to her British dignity. Now they were on our doorstep.

'Oh, lor,' said Mum, taking the carrots I had been slicing and putting them into the big saucepan. 'I wonder what they are like?'

'Just like our boys, Lal,' said Grampy: 'far from home, wounded and sick. It is a hospital, you know. Think how our lads are over there amongst foreigners and then think how we should be towards these lads.' He handed me a toffee from his apron pocket, which was my reward for helping. 'It could be worse: they could have built that place for prisoners. Think of that.'

'Prisoners, Grampy?' I wiped my hands on a tea towel. 'Prisoners?'

'Of course, prisoners – Italians, Germans. Got to put them somewhere, haven't we?'

Mum leant back against the wall. 'Whatever next? I ask,' she said. 'What a terrible thing this war is! What a place to bring kids up! Prisoners running about all over the place!'

'I shouldn't think they'll be doing any such thing,' said Grampy with a smile. 'They'll be kept safely locked away till this little fracas is over, then they'll be sent back to their families – as will our boys.'

'Oh, the poor things!' I said.

'Nan! They are our enemies,' said Mum.

'Not them – I meant *our* soldiers.'

I watched Grampy filling the chicken pot with the vegetable peelings and lighting the gas under it. All the scraps were boiled up and mixed with evil-smelling meal for chicken feed, and I knew that before long the house would reek with the sickly smell. I made my escape.

'Come on,' I shouted to Annie, who was leaning out of a bedroom window trying to reach up into the guttering to retrieve a ball. 'Let's go and see the Yanks.'

She was down like a flash, banging the front door as she emerged. We flew down through the dell, over the stream at the bottom, squelching through the black oozing mud into the Horses' Field beyond. Both of the animals turned their heads lazily and watched us as we scrambled up the steep field and through the wire fencing out on to the flat field, where fodder was grown for the cows at White's farm.

There were already several of the kids from the street pressed up against the high chain-link fencing surrounding the hospital, and a few red-dressing-gowned figures were talking to them.

Ivor Saunders waved his arm to us. 'Look what I've got,' he shouted: 'chewing gum.'

'Hi, kids,' said a voice, and along came a white-helmeted soldier in an unfamiliar uniform. He carried a stick and warned the men in red not to get too close to the wires.

'He's a century,' whispered Annie in my ear. 'He guards them.'

He seemed a very nice 'century' and gave us some gum in long, thin packets and a tube of sweets called 'Lifesavers', and we loved to hear him talk.

We had not tasted anything quite like them for a long, long time and mmm-ed and aahed as we champed away. Some of the men in the red dressing gowns sauntered over and joined in the conversation, too, and we mimicked their accents and asked greedily for more gum, 'for my little sister at home' and 'for my mum', with no intentions of handing it over when we did go home, but rather to satisfy our long-neglected sweet tooth.

At home we enthused over our new neighbours.

'They're ever so nice,' I told Mum as we laid the table for tea. 'They talk all funny, like on the pictures, and they gave us chewing gum.'

'Now, don't you get taking things from them,' said Mum sternly.

She rattled teaspoons into saucers and spooned some jam from a large jar of home-made into a little glass dish. Usually, if we were the only ones there the big jar would be plonked in the middle of the table.

'Is someone coming to tea?' I asked, eyeing the pretty dish.

'Not to tea,' she answered, 'but there is someone coming to see Dad, and they might just call as we are eating.'

No one called during the meal, but almost as soon as we had finished there was a knock at the door and we children were banished to the kitchen to do the washing-up. We stood in a huddle just inside the door, all eager to hear what was going on, but we couldn't hear a word. And then whoever it was was taken into the sitting room – the best room.

'Not more Vackies!' exclaimed John.

'Shouldn't think so,' I said, 'not with Gran and Gramps still here.'

Susan, her arms in the sink, said, 'Perhaps Barda's coming back. That would be nice.'

'She wouldn't want the best room; and anyway, who is it in there?'

'It's a man's voice,' said John, his ear to the connecting wall.

'I heard a woman when they came,' I said.

We were soon to know. Joan spilled the beans without even realising it.

'Are we having it, then?' she asked Dad when she arrived home, hot and sweaty from her bike ride from work.

'Having what?' Immediately John, Susan and I were interested.

'Another dog?' asked John.

'Trust you to spoil it,' Dad said to Joan, but he was smiling as he did so.

'Oh, come on, Dad – tell us,' we pleaded.

'Wait till tomorrow.'

He opened his *Evening Star* and shook it, settling down to read.

We clung round him, saying 'Please, Dad' and 'Go on, tell us' until he could bear it no longer.

He put the paper down and said, 'It's all Grampy Ward's fault. He says that our Nan ought to learn to play the piano – so I've bought one.'

We stood in shocked amazement.

John was first to speak: 'Is that all?' he said. 'I'm going out.' And he went.

'What do you think, Nan?' asked Mum, coming in from the bathroom, where she had been battling with Pat. 'Won't it be nice? You are going to have proper lessons, too.'

'But who were those people?' I asked.

'Fred Lygoe and his wife. They are going to pick it up for us tomorrow and just wanted to make sure that it would go through the doors and things.'

A piano! I couldn't believe it. Gran and Grampy were round at Auntie Enid's house for the day, but I couldn't wait to tell them, so I sped off leaving Mum's 'Hey, it's nearly bedtime' trailing behind me like vapour.

John was sitting on the grass with a gang of his friends, and as I raced by they all began the usual chant of 'Annie, Annie, any onny sin our Annie' and 'Nan, Nan, Finackapan', but this time I didn't stop to retort; I ran as fast as I could towards Dene Road.

Evelyn Plotts, who lived a few doors from Auntie, was in her front garden helping her 'auntie' with some gardening. She smiled at me and her 'auntie' said, 'Where's the fire?'

So I shouted, 'I've got to tell Grampy I'm having a piano.'

I knew Evelyn from church. She had been evacuated from London and the lady she called her auntie, Mrs Quartermain, was a lovely soul. Sometimes, ungrateful wretch that I must have been, I quite envied Evelyn for having found such a kind and welcoming home. She had arrived, like so many others, with nothing more than she stood up in, but Mrs Quartermain, who had no children of her own, had given her a lovely home with all the clothes and toys that she wanted. Their house was nice, too, with a long, interesting garden. On the odd occasions when Evelyn and I had walked home from church together we had spent many a pleasant afternoon or evening in that garden, lying on the lawn and peering up through the leaves of the cherry trees. But, in spite of all that, she had not become a special friend, like Sheila and Annie or even Joy.

Grampy was as pleased as I at the news and, although I suspected that he already knew all about it, he made out for my sake, I suppose, that it was all new to him. All the way home he kept saying things like 'Well I never' and 'My, oh my!' But something in the way he said them told me that he had been in on it from the start.

It was just after the piano arrived (and what a beautiful thing it was) and I had been enrolled for lessons in Old Headington, but had not yet started, that Mum said that she had been told that we had to be friendly to the Yanks at the Churchill, and as they were wounded and a long way from home we should invite them for tea on Sundays and generally make them welcome. Dad thought it was a terrible idea, what with the rationing and the fact that really they were foreigners and we knew nothing about them. Of course, we kids didn't agree. The thought of all the chewing gum going to someone else's house! But Dad was adamant and although several of the families in the street had one or two of these homesick young lads for Sunday dinner, or Saturday supper, we didn't.

Rex Pollard waved a chocolate bar under my nose: 'Look what our Yank gave us,' he taunted.

And Brian Brockall tore open a colourful tube of Lifesavers – small round boiled sweets with a hole in the middle, like a lifebelt – grinning at me as he popped them one by one into his mouth, scrunching noisily to make me all the more envious.

'Got 'em from our Yank,' he said.

Despite our constant whining and nagging, Mum and Dad were adamant, backed up, of course, by Gran.

Then, one cold Sunday afternoon, down the street came two Americans, walking along deep in conversation, and while we watched from the window Mrs Brockall called out to them. They hesitated, and then made their way across to her gate. They all talked for a while, then, to our horror, one of them went into the house and the other, uncertain whether to continue with his walk or to turn back, took a packet of cigarettes from his pocket, lit one and turned on his heel.

'Did you see that?' asked Mum angrily. 'That blessed woman only asked one in – oh, that poor chap.' She watched, with a sorrowful expression on her face, as he retreated slowly. 'Go and ask him in for tea, Nan.'

I needed no second bidding. I was off, and caught him before he reached the flats.

'Mum says would you like to come to tea?' I gasped.

He looked a little taken aback, but smiled, said he'd love to and accompanied me back to the house.

And so Eddie came into our lives. He was tall, slim and very good-looking, and we all took to him right from the start. Dad, aroused from his Sunday afternoon nap in the armchair with the *News of the World* covering his face, was startled to see this newcomer in our midst, seated at the table, his elbows on the thick red cloth, a little shy, but gradually warming to our eager questions. He told us that he was from South Carolina, didn't like to be called 'Yankee' and the fact that we were about to have tea at half past four simply fascinated him. It seemed that at home they had breakfast, lunch, and dinner in the evening. That to us was absolutely ridiculous! Eating at that time of night, a full-blown meal, would surely give anyone terrible nightmares!

After that first meeting he became a regular visitor, delighting Mum with his gifts – jars of coffee, packets of sugar lumps, tins of meat and, best of all for us kids, packets of 'cookies' and bags of sweets – or 'candies', as Eddie called them. He made a game of it, not just handing them out, but hiding them all over the room, under cushions, behind the curtains, even in our shoes in the little brown-painted cupboard where they lived. He would also use them as a surreptitious bribe when Mum asked for someone to wash up after a meal. To our negative response, Eddie would hold up a 'candy bar' out of Mum's sight and just raise his eyebrows. Mum got her 'volunteers'.

Yes, I must say, Eddie was soon like one of the family, and the mystery surrounding someone from America, like all wonderful things to children, soon settled down and he just seemed like another cousin. So we turned our interests elsewhere, and as usual it was John who came home with more news.

'Guess what?' He sat down heavily on the chair opposite me at the table.

I sighed, 'What?' and didn't even bother to look up from my books.

'There's Eyeties up the Ridings!'

'What's Eyeties?' I licked my fingers and turned a page. 'What's French for fish?' Doing John's homework was a good way to learn French.

'*Poison*,' he offered. 'Up the Ridings they are – 'undreds of 'em.'

I studied his French vocabulary, dog-eared and grubby from much thumbing.

'It's *poisson*.' I looked at him, at his wide grey eyes. 'Hundreds of what?'

'Eyeties. I keep telling you – Italian prisoners of war.' He said it slowly and deliberately, smiled and stood up. 'Wanna come and see?'

Homework forgotten, we raced for our bikes and cycled like mad things to the end of the road. By the flats, astride their bikes, chattering eagerly, were the rest of the gang: Mick Smith, Tim Jones, Ivor Saunders, Johnny Winters, Len Jeffs, Annie and Sheila. They pushed off when they saw us coming, and we pedalled furiously out on to the Slade (which was the main road up to the roundabout at Wingfield Hospital), straight round it and up Old Road towards Shotover.

By this time the boys were way out in front, Ivor bent low over his handlebars, his red knees pumping like pistons, the V-shaped gusset in the back of his trousers on show to us all. Tim Jones was riding his big brother's bike and had to stand on the pedals all the way because he couldn't reach the saddle. Sheila puffed and panted along beside me on Kathleen's bike, which had a mackintosh cover stretched over the back wheel, to stop the rider's skirts getting in the spokes, and a tattered old basket on the front, held in place with one strap and a piece of bootlace. It rattled and bounced along with Sheila going up and down like a cork on the water, her hair streaming out behind her like a witch. Annie had the reverse. She had got hold of someone's bike, but I didn't know whose. It was obviously for someone much younger, because she seemed to be sitting on the road she was so low. Her head was barely level with my elbow and she had to pedal three times as fast as anyone else to keep up. Her knees were up under her chin, showing her dark-green fleecy-lined drawers, her brow furrowed in concentration and her hair like a bird's nest.

We turned into the Ridings, which was a tarmacked lane off to the right just before the steep ascent on to Shotover Plain. By the time we girls arrived the boys had thrown down their bikes and were creeping Indian-style into the undergrowth beneath the trees. They signalled with waves of their hands for us to be quiet and keep low, so we did. I crawled along on my hands and knees, getting a face-ful of Sheila's backside every time she hesitated; and Annie, in turn, received the same from me. The ground was a bit oozy here and there and I noted with some consternation that the white sleeves of my school blouse were no longer so. At last the crawling line stopped and one by one we edged up to where Mick and Ivor lay.

'Where are they?' I whispered.

Mick said nothing, just pointed.

There were several wooden huts in a sort of clearing, surrounded by a high wire fence with barbed wire on the top. Some men in dull grey and khaki clothes were wandering about in twos and threes, and a few were sitting with their backs to the sides of the huts, chatting. Sheila was disappointed.

'They're only men,' she said, pouting.

'They're prisoners of war,' said Ivor in a hoarse whisper.

'Shouldn't they be chained up or something?' asked Annie.

I got the feeling that she would have liked it better if they were chained and hung from the walls so that their feet couldn't quite touch the ground.

'My dad says that they are working at White's farm, helping out.' Tim pulled at a piece of grass and sucked the end.

I looked at the wire. It didn't seem very strong.

'Let's go,' I whispered.

'Scaredy-cat,' said John. 'They won't hurt you. They've got guards and things.'

'I can't see any,' said Sheila, peering through the dock leaves and nettles.

'Well, there are some – somewhere.' Mick looked round carefully. 'I think we'd better go before someone sees us.'

We began to crawl back through the undergrowth, then, fear lending speed, we were up and running, crashing through brambles and nettles back to where the tangle of bikes lay. With tugging, pulling and a few bad words we all gained possession of a vehicle and were up in the saddles and whizzing off for the safety of 'our street'.

Worse was to follow. Not long after our trip to the Eyeties' camp, Dad came in from cleaning out the henhouse.

'There are Germans at the bottom of our garden,' he said, just like that.

Mum dropped the pile of saucers she was carrying into the washing-up bowl with a splosh.

'Oh, whatever next, Ted?' she asked. Her face looked white and drawn. 'Haven't we got enough to put up with? I ask you! Germans! How can I let these kids out to play with all these foreigners running wild all over the place?'

Dad smiled. 'They're hardly running loose, Lal,' he said. 'They're sitting there having a rest. They've been clearing out the stream down the bottom. I thought you might make them a jug of tea or something?'

'Not on your life! Make them a jug of tea? With our rations? No!'

She turned her back on him and put some Oxydol into the copper. It was washing day and a mountain of dirty clothes covered the floor of the kitchen, where she had been sorting them into piles.

Dad filled the kettle and lifted down the big blue-and-white jug from the shelf.

'What're you doing?' Mum was suspicious.

'Making them some tea. They're only boys and they have nothing except some bread and cheese.'

'Cheese! Cheese!' said Mum. 'And we can't get it for love nor money.'

The tea was made and Dad carried the steaming jug and two tin mugs down the path towards the end of the garden. I followed at a distance. I desperately wanted to see these terrible men, but thought it best that I kept Dad's wide back between me and them.

Sitting in the long grass, leaning against our fence, were eight or nine young men. They were, as Dad had said, very young. They wore greyish-green jackets and trousers with a big 'P.O.W.' painted on the back and little caps with long peaks. They were a little surprised when Dad gestured towards the guard – an American soldier with a gun! – but he allowed them to drink the tea, and Dad even handed out some of his Woodbines! 'Tailor-mades', as Dad called them, were his only luxury. It was cheaper to roll his own, and cigarettes were very hard to get hold of. Betty had brought him these on her last leave and I felt very proud that Dad should offer them to these pale young men.

One of them, who wore a little silver crucifix in his cap, said 'Thank you' very carefully in English, and they smiled and nodded.

The guard watched as the mugs were passed round between them; then when it was all gone he collected the jug and handed it back to Dad.

'Thanks,' he said, 'but don't make a habit of it!'

'Pig!' I thought.

CHAPTER 12

We saw a great deal of the Germans after this. They worked in Bury Knowle Park, trimming the flower beds, which were not very large at this time because every spare bit of ground had to be used to grow vegetables and everyone was 'digging for victory', as the posters told us to. Still, in the park there were one or two tiny beds and they made a welcome sight as everyone's garden contained nothing more than rows and rows of potatoes and suchlike. These same POWs were set to work repairing the public toilets by the gates, and we would encounter them in the queues at the cake shop, where we stood patiently waiting for the doors to open.

Sponge cakes and buns were available, but only one cake or six buns per person. Mum sent John and me to queue up one Saturday and we stood one behind the other to obtain two cakes. The lady in her little blue cotton cap and apron served me first, then John stepped up and asked for the same type of sponge. She looked at me, stuffing my purchase into the shopping bag, looked at John, smiled and handed him his. Being young and a bit naive, he immediately tried to put it into my bag. I cottoned on straight away that she knew we were together and desperately tried to prevent him doing so. The cake landed jam-side down on the shop floor and several of the women in the queue were heard to whisper 'Shocking' and 'Greedy' and things like that. Outside I stalked ahead of John, who, battered cake in his hand, ran along behind, quite unaware that everyone knew we had been discovered in our deception. We were like two peas in a pod, and to try to pretend that we were not together was absolutely ludicrous! I arrived home in a terrible temper, and was not pacified by Mum's laughter and her belated advice.

'You should have gone in quite separately,' she said. 'Looking at you two, no one could have been fooled. I'd have thought you would have had more sense.' She took the cake that John had dropped, scraped the jam off and put it in the cake tin. 'It'll be OK,' she said. 'I'll put some more jam on it.'

I was furious still. I glared at John.

'And don't you ever come shopping with me again,' I said.

In this same shop I encountered a German POW waiting patiently for his turn, but each time another lady joined the queue he would step aside to let her in front. I bought the two buns I had been sent to get for Joan and Mr Woods, who was her boss in the Co-op shoe shop opposite, and I found myself feeling deeply sorry for this young man. He was getting nowhere and as I watched, clutching the buns, the assistant put up the 'Sold Out' board, and he went away empty-handed. I ran across the road to the shoe shop and burst in, gabbling away about it.

Joan, in her usual soft-hearted way, was as upset as I was.

'Oh, the poor chap,' she said, going to the door. 'Where did he go?'

I was near to tears. 'Down towards the park,' I said.

'I'm going to take him my bun,' she said.

Mr Woods came out from the back of the shop. He had heard what I had had to say.

'Don't be silly, Miss Hathaway,' he said, blinking behind his little wire-rimmed spectacles. 'You can't do a thing like that. What would people think?' He tugged his jacket down – an irritating habit of his. 'That would be fraternising – and you know what people think of *that*!'

'But he didn't get anything to eat, Mr Woods,' I said.

'Then that's too bad. After all, they are the enemy, aren't they? And the food in our shops should be for us – not them.'

'But—' Joan began, her cheeks turning red.

'No – buts are not necessary. You let the authorities take care of their needs. Cakes indeed!'

He tugged again and went back into his little curtained-off cubbyhole of an office.

Sheila Morris, the other assistant, grimaced after him.

'Miserable old devil,' she whispered.

When we left at lunchtime we purposely went past the park so that I could show Joan which one it was. They were piling stones by the toilets, and I am sorry to say that they all looked alike to me, so I pointed unobtrusively to one that I thought looked most like him. He glanced at us, and he must have been wondering why these three young ladies smiled benignly at him with pity in their eyes. He half smiled back.

That made us feel better, and out of earshot Sheila said, 'Isn't he good-looking?'

Joan just smiled, her eyes soft and dreamy.

At home Pat and Susan were playing with a strange-looking toy – a little wooden thing in the shape of a table-tennis bat with strings threaded through so that they hung underneath with a wooden weight on the end. On the bat were four wooden chickens, and by moving it in a circular motion these would peck in turn – peck, peck, peck – moving their heads up and down. I was fascinated by this and asked for a go.

'Where did you get it?' I asked, mesmerised by the bobbing hens.

'Them Germans who drink our tea,' said Pat.

Dad confirmed it. 'They made it for you children in return for the jug of tea the other day,' he said. 'Isn't it lovely?'

'And look what I've got,' said Grampy, coming in from the kitchen.

I could see nothing in his hands.

'What?' I enquired.

He lifted one foot. On it was a rope slipper, woven out of string, beautifully made and decorated with a pompom of green string.

'Ooh, aren't they nice?' I enthused.

I rather hoped that there would be a pair for me somewhere, but nobody made a move to get them so I had to assume that I had none. However, just a few days afterwards a pair just my size was handed over the bottom fence. I put them on and ran along to see Sheila, who was chalking a 'snail hopscotch' on the concrete outside her back door.

She studied my rope-encased feet carefully for a moment or two, pushed back her frizzy fringe from her forehead and said, 'Them Germans down the neller make 'em?'

(It seems that Mrs Tanner – a sweet little Cockney lady, and now a permanent lodger with the Williamses – had quite a few variations for our more familiar words. To her the dell was the neller.)

I nodded and raised a foot for her to see the intricate workmanship.

'Mrs Tanner says we shouldn't have nothin' to do with 'em.' Sheila concentrated on her chalking. 'They are prisoners of war!' She almost whispered the statement and selected another piece of chalk from the little pile by the step. 'Wanna play hopscotch?'

I watched her for a moment or two as she moved her arm in a wide circle round herself, marking out the 'steps' in a spiral, shuffling round on her bottom as she did so.

'No,' I said.

I was disappointed that she had not enthused over my slippers and was even more annoyed that as I made my way homeward again one of the dratted things kept falling off. I wriggled my foot back into it, peering over my shoulder to make sure that Sheila wasn't watching, but she was still in her back garden and the side gate was shut. I walked on, taking care not to raise the foot with the loose slipper too high off the ground.

During the days of the POWs, we collected quite a few toys and knick-knacks, mostly made from bits and pieces, but all beautifully done. One of my favourites was a whistle cut from a piece of wood. It had several holes along its length; and although I could never master the idea of lifting and lowering my fingers as I blew, to get a tune, to my annoyance Sheila could and the tunes were recognisable. Annie was almost as good and wanted one for herself, so we thought up how to get another. We met in the alley between Annie's house and Ivor Saunders' house, and into a hanky (paper bags were very scarce) we put an apple, two rock cakes (taken from Mum's cooling tray when she wasn't looking) and three Woodbines (taken from Annie's brother's jacket pocket while he was in the other room). We peered at the spoils.

'Don't look very much, do it?' said Annie.

'No,' I had to agree, and I didn't think much of the grubby hanky either, but I didn't like to say so, because Annie had got that. 'We need more.'

In our larder, on a plate, were three cold cooked sausages. Obviously, Mr Rolfe had been round. I waited till everyone was out of the way, took one of them, stuffed it up my sleeve and ran out. Annie was delighted. The poor lonely sausage joined the other bits and pieces and we set off to find whereabouts in the dell the prisoners were working. They were down by the stream, clearing the long stringy weeds from the water. The guard – an American – regarded us with suspicion as we approached, and the Germans took the opportunity to straighten their backs for a while. The American gestured to them to get on with their work and took a step towards us.

'What d'you want, kids?' he asked, his jaws moving rapidly as he chewed his gum.

'We've brought this for the Germans,' said Annie, holding out the pathetic little bundle. He took it from her and unwrapped it, his face devoid of all expression as he examined the contents. His jaws didn't stop.

'OK,' he said.

And that was it. The prisoners carried on working, and the guard turned his back on us. Annie looked at me and I looked at her.

She mouthed, 'What about my whistle?' and I shrugged my shoulders in reply.

We stood for a while not quite knowing what to do. Should we ask for it? Neither of us could pluck up the courage, so we turned and made our way back to the top of the hill. Mick Smith and David Robins were wheeling their bikes down the track.

'Your Dad'll bash you for talking to them Germans,' said David. He was a tall pale-faced boy, some years older than us. 'You keep away from 'em.'

'Who's going to tell?' said Annie.

'I will if I see you down there again,' said David.

'Telltale tit, your tongue shall be split,' taunted Annie, and she began to run out of swiping distance.

'Cheeky young bugger,' said David, and they continued on their way, steering their bikes between the tall grass towards the wider piece of track, which was a favourite location for riding at full pelt all the way to the bottom.

When we reached the path at the top we turned just in time to see both of them tearing down with their legs out on each side. It looked fun, but something we wouldn't like to do. It seemed quite hair-raising to us.

The rest of the day was spent in Annie's back garden. There wasn't much to do out there because it was just a sea of mud where the ducks were allowed to wander anywhere they had a mind to – even, on occasions, into the kitchen, only to be chased out again by a red-faced Mrs Whaley, waving her big red arms in anger.

We sat on the dustbins and talked.

'Mean sods,' said Annie. 'Mean buggers.'

Her use of 'naughty language' never ceased to amaze me. Here in her own back garden, in earshot of the open kitchen window, where I could see through the clouds of steam, from the washing, her brother, she was swearing like a trooper. No one in our house swore like that. I heard Dad say 'bloody' in the shed once, but other things were never said, and certainly not by us children. John would sometimes slip up with an odd word and I know that he swore sometimes out in the street, but if he was heard he had a swift clip across the ear. The kids in the corner 'Vackie house' swore even worse. Even the littlest one, Dawn, barely four years old at this time, used *bleedin'* and *bastard* quite freely.

Here was Annie giving vent to her feelings about the ingratitude of the POWs, feeling very hurt that she hadn't been handed a whistle after all our efforts. She kicked out at a passing duck.

'I ain't givin' 'em nuffin' else,' she vowed.

When I got home later Mum was looking very stern. She was doing the ironing, and by the way the iron was thumped down after each bit I knew at once something was wrong.

'Take those up and put them in Gran's room,' she said, pointing to a pile of clothes, neatly ironed and folded. 'And don't scrump them up.'

I did as I was bid. Gran and Grampy were out, probably up at the library, so I laid them carefully on a chair and went downstairs again. Mum's mouth was still set in a firm line. I knelt on the horsehair sofa under the window and peered out.

'Start laying the table – it'll be teatime shortly,' said Mum, shaking out a pillowcase.

I did as I was bid, still not able to think what could be wrong. I soon found out.

When the others filed in for tea, Mum said, 'Right, before we sit down there's something I must know.' She studied the row of faces before her. 'Which of you has been in the larder and took a sausage from the plate there?'

There was a stony silence.

'There were three; now there are two.'

'Are you sure there were three, Lal?' asked Grampy.

Mum nodded. 'Three!' she confirmed. She took the plate from the larder. On it were the two remaining sausages and in the fat was the unmistakable shape of another. 'See?' she said.

I could feel my cheeks burning, but I said nothing and kept my eyes firmly on a chipped tile at the side of the sink.

'Wasn't me,' said John.

'Nor me,' said Sue.

'I wouldn't take it – I don't like sausages,' said little Pat.

'I didn't,' I lied. 'What would I want with a sausage?'

All through tea we children were lectured on dishonesty and greed, on the need for everyone to be scrupulously fair as regards food and so on. I chewed my bread and Bovril and listened to it all and thought how unfair this world was when I had committed such a dreadful crime – and Annie still hadn't got her whistle.

CHAPTER 13

The Yanks were everywhere. They walked about in Oxford as if they owned the place and Holyoak Hall in Headington was abuzz with them at weekends when they held the Saturday-night hops. We would congregate at the end of the road about half past six to watch the parade of older girls making their way towards Headington, their high-heeled shoes clicking on the pavements as they passed, and the smell of their Evening in Paris hanging on the air behind them.

'Blimey, what a pong,' we would chorus, holding our noses and grimacing.

'Going Yankee-bashing?'

'Bring us back some gum.'

The lipsticked, peroxided girls would merely toss their heads and stalk on, pretending they hadn't heard.

'My dad said they jitterbugger up there,' said Sheila, perching herself on the wall outside Joy's flat.

Mr Hillier scowled out from behind the curtains, but she put her thumb to her nose and he disappeared from view.

'What's that?' I asked.

'Ain't you never 'eard of jitterbugging?' asked Margaret Smith. She didn't normally speak this way, but on occasions, just to annoy Barbara, her older sister, who happened to be with us this time, she would lapse into the cross between Oxford and Cockney. 'It's dancing.'

'I saw them doing it on the news at the pictures,' Mick said, banging his bike lamp with a clenched fist. The bulb spurted a pale yellow glow, held it for a couple of seconds and went out. 'Bloody thing,' he said.

'Yes, so did I,' said Barbara. 'They go like mad, flinging each

133

other over their shoulders and everything. It's really good.'

'But you wouldn't go up the Holyoak, would you?' I asked. Somehow I couldn't see Barbara amongst all these highly painted girls.

She shook her head. 'My mum'd have a fit,' she said.

I looked at her closely. She was very dark and very pretty and I thought that perhaps the Yanks would like her to go.

'Would you go out with a Yank?' asked Annie. 'Our Helen said she would if she found a nice one.'

'Yuk,' Margaret said. 'I can't stand the way they champ away on that gum all the time. It makes me feel sick.'

'Some of them are quite nice,' I offered. 'Our Eddie's nice.'

'Oh, yes, he is,' said Barbara, 'but he hasn't been around lately, has he?'

Margaret nudged her arm. 'There you are – I told you that you went all gooey when he was about.' She giggled. 'You should see her – pretending not to notice, but watching from behind the curtains to see him.'

Barbara blushed deeply. 'No, I don't,' she argued. She picked up her cardigan, which was laid across the wall. 'I've got to go now,' she said, and walked off.

'Told you, told you,' Margaret taunted after her.

'Have you seen that one that goes into Brockall's?' asked Sheila. 'He's really ugly – all greasy hair and a brown face.'

'He's Italian or something,' said Ivor. 'A ruddy Eyetie.'

'They're our enemies,' I said, 'not Yanks.'

'This one's an Eyetie anyway,' said Ivor. He bent to have a go at Mick's bike lamp. 'You need a new bulb,' he said.

Mick aimed a kick at the bike and it fell with a crash. The glass fell out of the lamp and broke.

'Need a new lamp now,' laughed Sheila.

He lunged at her as she sat on the wall, pushing her backwards so that her hair almost touched the garden behind. She kicked and struggled.

'Sod off, Smithy,' she hollered.

'Look who's coming.' It was almost a hiss from Annie. 'It's that Vackie girl from the corner.'

It was indeed her. She wore a red dress that seemed several sizes too small and was far too short. Her legs were brown and streaked where she had obviously done the common trick of using gravy browning to stain them because stockings were practically non-existent. She had made a poor job of it though and it showed. Her shoes were black and very high-heeled and her hair was a ginger mop.

We stared as she drew near, none of us having the courage to speak. Rita was not one who took kindly to comments of any sort. Mick released his hold on the red-faced Sheila and we all stood in silence and watched as Rita wriggled past. Her cheap scent filled our nostrils and we pulled faces at each other.

'She's going, I bet,' whispered Annie.

'She's still at school. They won't let her in there,' said Ivor quietly.

'Whatya starin' at?' she snarled. 'Bugger off.'

'Dunno – it ain't got a label on,' said Annie with a sudden show of bravery.

Rita stopped in her tracks, turned and glared at us. 'I'd smash yer bleedin' faces in, all on yer, if I 'adn't got a date and wasn't all dressed up.'

We had all drawn back, just a little, from our previous positions. As I said, Rita did not take kindly to insults, but Mick, made bolder by her 'if', said, 'Got a date? What? You?'

She stood facing us, hands on her hips, her scarlet lips curled in a snarl.

'Yeah, any objections?'

Mick backed away. 'Yankee-basher,' he said.

She made a quick little run towards us and we scattered like scared rabbits.

In the safety of our back garden, Sheila, Annie and I crept down into the Anderson shelter and carefully closed the door. In the dark, musty confines we discussed the girls at Holyoak Hall, the Yanks who jitterbugged and Rita. She'd said she'd got a date! And her still at school! She was about to leave school soon, we knew, but to have a date and to go *there*!

The following day I went to Headington to get some shopping for Mum, and Joy came with me. I related all the events of the previous evening, embroidering a bit as I told them to make it more interesting. I told her that Rita had a date with an American, and he was a general and had picked her up in a great big car, but Joy didn't seem very shocked.

'They're quite nice, those Yanks,' she said.

'Well, our Eddie is,' I said, 'but not all of them. Most of them are only chasing the girls because they want to flirt around.'

'Our Rose is going out with one,' said Joy. She tossed her blonde hair in defiance and looked directly at me with her violet eyes.

I was aghast. Rose was her elder sister. She was quite a bit older than Joy and I had always thought her a very shy lady. Going out with a Yank! Rose couldn't be a Yankee-basher.

'He's ever such a nice man,' said Joy quietly. 'Even my dad likes him.'

Over dinner later I related this bit of news to the family. To my utter surprise no one seemed to think it terrible at all.

'Rose Hillier's a sensible girl,' said Mum, 'and I'm sure he's a decent chap.'

Eddie called in during the afternoon and brought Mum some more goodies for the cupboard and some 'cookies' for us kids. I stood looking at him and he gave me one of his lovely smiles.

'What's the matter with you?' he asked.

'Just looking,' I said.

'What's going on in that head of yours?' he asked. He seated himself in the corner of the sofa, and patted the seat by the side of him. 'Come here and tell me.'

I sat down.

'Eddie,' I began, 'you don't go jitterbuggering up at the Holyoak, do you?'

He laughed, showing his white teeth. 'No, I don't – and anyway the word is *jitterbugging*.' He ruffled my hair. 'Why should I want to go up there – the Holy what?'

'With those girls,' I said.

'I don't need to – I've got all I need here.' He looked over my shoulder. 'And here she comes.'

136

I turned my head. Joan was standing in the doorway, her pretty blue-striped summer dress and her white wedge-heeled shoes on, her jacket over her arm. She was smiling.

I stood up.

'You look lovely,' I said.

'Hi,' said Eddie.

He stood up, too, buttoning his tunic. He picked up his cap.

'Shall we go, princess?'

I stood open-mouthed and they went out – Joan and Eddie! I rushed to the window, kneeling on the old sofa so that I could watch them go up the road. How wonderful!

'Mum! Mum!' I shouted.

CHAPTER 14

I dutifully went every Tuesday, after school, into Old Headington for my music lessons, plonking away at the ivories under the stern gaze of an old harridan of a woman who relentlessly rapped my knuckles for every wrong note, and I sat at home for an hour every day practising all she had told me and vowing to 'get her' one day.

'When I'm grown-up!' I would say to myself as I ploughed through the scales.

Sometimes, as I sat in our best room, the door would open quietly and Mum would peer round, smile and join me on the stool. She would teach me little duets, which were much more fun than that old dragon's lessons. Mum could play beautifully, but by ear. I only had to say the name of a popular song and she would hum a little of it to herself and immediately play it. I was enthralled. Perhaps if I managed to put up with the old gorgon I would one day be able to do this. It gave me encouragement to carry on. Mum seemed pleased with my progress and would sit back with her eyes closed and a little smile on her face, her arms wrapped in her apron while I went through 'The Bluebells of Scotland' and 'The Little Match Girl' over and over again. I was very happy when I graduated to 'Hungarian Dance' and she clapped her hands as I finished without a fault.

Of course, I was missing precious playing time, and time and again as I plugged away I heard the knock, knock of one of my friends and I'd hear Mum or Dad saying, 'No, sorry – she's practising.'

It became a chore and I tried every trick in the book to escape to play for a few hours. If Eddie was there he would wave a candy bar at me and point to the back room. If I went in to practise, the bar would be mine. Of course Mum didn't know about these little bribes, and indeed if she had Eddie would have been in trouble with her. It was our little secret and it worked. I have always been a pushover for a chocolate bar!

Then came the day of the letter. This was quite different from letters from Barda. It was addressed to me, but in a brown envelope, and Dad opened it.

'I know what this is,' he said with a smile at me.

I waited with bated breath. Perhaps it was my turn to join up. No, not at eleven years old, surely!

'You've passed,' said Dad. 'Look, Lal.'

He passed it to Mum, who read it slowly.

'You've got a place at Oxford Central Girls' School,' she said.

John had passed the eleven-plus and was already a pupil at Oxford City Boys' High School, and now it seemed I was going to Central. I raced along to Sheila's house. She had taken the eleven-plus at the same time and she must have passed. She was cleverer than me.

She had, but her parents had told her that she could not go to the grammar school as they could not afford it. I was very upset and told Mum that I didn't want to go either. But they were adamant about it and I had to go. I would be starting in the September. It was May – Dad's birthday.

Sheila and I sat on the roof of her shed discussing our future apart. Annie had not passed and she would be going to the senior school up the road from our junior school in Margaret Road – with Sheila and Joy and Eileen and Margaret, and everyone in the world, it seemed, except me. I was very down and picked at the flaking rust on the roof.

'Wish I hadn't passed now,' I said.

'We'll still be able to play in the evenings.' Annie's voice was comforting, but she was overjoyed that she was able to leave The Poplars and join the gang.

'Bet you'll have lots of homework and stuff,' said Sheila.

'John does,' I said.

'If you have homework and practising you'll never be out.'

Sheila was the voice of doom. She lay back and stared up at the sky. 'And it's going to rain.'

Annie gave her a little punch and she scowled at her.

'Well, it is,' she said.

Suddenly the back door opened and Mrs Williams appeared. She was red-faced and beaming.

'It's over,' she shouted. 'The war's over.'

We looked at each other in disbelief. Then, in almost one movement, we were off the shed, not even stopping to grope with our toes for the rim of the water butt, but falling in a giggling heap on the hard earth. I fled homewards, only to find that the family had obviously already heard the news. They were hugging each other and laughing and crying, Grampy doing a version of the Highland fling and whirling Gran round and round. Even dear old Paddy was barking.

When the hysteria faded, Susan said quite seriously, 'Can I have some sweets now?' And everyone dissolved into laughter again.

Within days there was talk of street parties, and banners appeared at windows welcoming returning soldiers. Mrs Brockall's Yank was sent packing and Brian and Derek had their dad home again.

'When's our party?' we children asked 1,000 times a day, to be told 'Soon' and 'Not long now' and 'Wait and see', and it wasn't until I saw Mr King on his knees at the Bulan Place end of our road, chalking 'Road Closed – Party in Progress', that I knew the day had come.

Bunting was stretched from lamp post to lamp post – those poor redundant lamp posts that hadn't held a glimmer for so long were dressed over all, although the lights still could not be lit. That joy was to come.

Union Jacks flew from all the windows up and down the street, and we children were sent off to build a bonfire: 'Get all the stuff you can.'

The men, clambering about on ladders and chairs to get the decorations up, shouted instructions like sergeant majors, and for once in our lives we didn't argue. Off down the dell we raced, dragging every bush and branch that would move, back up the hill to the waste ground at the end of the road.

It seemed that the world and his wife visited us at some time during the day with anything that would burn, and quite a lot of stuff that wouldn't. Tables and chairs were piled on and we scoured the houses for junk. Mrs Horwood brought out an old overstuffed armchair, struggling along, half dragging it until one of the boys saw her and went to help. We heaved and shoved and got it fairly safely on top. Then when it was completed we stood back and admired our handywork. It was good. It was very good, and very big.

'What we want is an 'Itler to go in the chair,' said Mick Smith.

A huge cheer rang out and we all went off to find suitable things with which to make one. The grown-ups were very co-operative and soon he was finished. Annie wanted to put him up there straight away, but it was too high so we agreed to wait until some of the men could help.

'After dinner,' said Mick, who was always hungry. 'I'm going to have my dinner.'

'Yeah, and me,' said someone else, and we all drifted off home.

Disaster met our eyes when we returned. The whole thing had collapsed and lay around like an enormous rubbish tip. Hitler was upside down under the upturned armchair.

'Look what some bugger's done to our fire,' said Johnny Winters. 'I bet it was those kids from Fairview.'

Fairview was another estate not far away, and sometimes our boys had a scrap or two with them: a few shouted insults and a bloody nose or two, nothing much. It was hard to believe that they would do this. We set about rebuilding, and before long everything was back as before and old Hitler was sitting on the top after a lot of humping and shoving by Mr Saunders and Mr Jeffs.

Back in the street the women had laid out long lines of tables, each donated by a family, covered them with clean sheets and were in the process of carrying out trays of sandwiches and cakes and jugs of lemonade. Pale stuff it was, made with awful bitter-tasting lemonade powder from Bowls' shop. It gave you a saffron-coloured tongue and a sore throat, but was drunk in great quantities to augment our meagre sweet rations. It made a passable drink, though, and the sight of all those big jugs of it made our mouths water deliciously, and the plates of food made us realise how long ago dinner had been. We were all dispatched to get chairs and plates and a mug each, and in no time at all we were all seated and, like locusts, the tables were cleared in double-quick time by our grabbing hands. With jam round our mouths and lemonade staining our fronts, we laughed and giggled and shouted, while the grown-ups drank glasses of beer and giggled like teenagers.

A crowd of Americans joined us and the tables were pushed back on to the pavements so that the dancing could begin. And such dancing there was! The two women from the corner house led the whole street in 'The Lambeth Walk', everyone taking a great delight in the 'OY!', then into 'Horsey-Horsey, Don't You Stop'. The Yanks thought this great fun and begged again and again for it. Mr Gardner's gramophone really worked overtime, and every time the spring started to run down, and the music got slower and slower, there were squeals of panic for someone to wind it up, and once more the music picked up speed and we were off again.

'They're going to light the bonny!' shouted someone, and we were all carried along by the crowd to the waste ground. Mr King was there with his son, Norman, each with a lighted twist of newspaper, poking it in at various points around the base of the pile. To a great cheer from all of us, a great tongue of flame leapt up through the branches and she was away! The sparks lunged themselves up into the darkening sky and the pungent smoke drifted away like ghosts, ever changing in shape. I stood with my arms round Sheila, our mouths open in awe. It was the best bonfire ever.

A man's voice started singing 'God Save the King', and we all joined in. I could feel a lump in my throat and my eyes began to prickle. I wiped them with my sleeve.

Mr Rolfe, standing by, smiled at me. 'Smoke in your eyes?' he said softly. 'Mine too.'

'Old 'Itler's 'ad it now,' shouted a voice from the far side of the inferno, and everyone laughed and cheered as the flames caught the dummy and the chair burnt fiercely, toppling sideways and tipping it out.

We children jumped up and down, clapping our hands in glee.

At last we were getting our own back for all those years of war. It was a small vengeance, but to us it was a mighty blow of defiance.

We formed ourselves into three enormous circles, one inside the other, and encircled the fire, singing all the songs we could think of as the fire crackled, spat and hissed, reddening our faces and warming us.

'When the Lights Go On Again' we sang and 'There'll Be Bluebirds Over' and 'Roll out the Barrel' and 'The Long and the Short and the Tall'. And as the fire dwindled we formed a long conga line and danced our way back into the street. The men had fixed up a Tannoy outside Mr King's house, and the music was blaring from inside. The Vackie woman, her hair tied up in a turban, sang 'Paper Doll' over the microphone, with a drunken Yank hanging round her neck. She was quite tone-deaf, and when she finished everyone cheered and called for more so that we could enjoy the torture further. Mr Brockall gave us a rendering of 'In a Monastery Garden', with all the birdsong whistled though his fingers, and several of the children sang in pining voices, crackling out over the air.

As the night wore on and everyone became tired and more than just a little tipsy, the music on the gramophone slowed and the dancing became more of a shuffle than a gallop. The debris of red, white and blue paper hats and streamers blew gently about the dancers' feet and became entangled with their legs. Heads lay on shoulders and dancing became a gentle rocking motion. I sat on one of the tables with Annie and Sheila, leaning back against Mr Fleetwood's hedge, and no one spoke. Our heads nodded sleepily. It was quite dark now because there were still no street lights and on some of the tables were lanterns casting pale orange circles of light on to the crumpled sheets and weird shadows from the piles of empty mugs and plates, forlornly cast aside now that they were empty. My eyes closed and I could hear Sheila breathing gently as she slept beside me. There was no sound from Annie, so I assumed that she was asleep too.

Suddenly I was aware of a voice saying, 'Here she is!' and I opened my eyes to see George, Annie's brother, standing before us with someone else. As my eyes became aware I could make out the figure of someone in a sailor's uniform. It was Billy, her older brother! What excitement then! Annie squealed with delight when she saw him and leapt at him, hugging him and kissing him all over his beaming face.

'Billy, Billy,' she kept saying, the tears pouring down her face.

Everyone else, suddenly awakened by the commotion, left the dancing and crowded round, shaking his hand and handing out more glasses of beer. The chattering and laughter grew and grew and the whole party got going again. It was wonderful! Mrs Whaley, so happy to see her son again, cried into her apron (she was never without her apron and, VE party or not, she was not going to take it off now). The older girls fussed around Billy, who was dark and very handsome, and he was enjoying every moment of their attention; and Annie hung on to his sleeve and wouldn't let him out of her sight.

It was after midnight before Dad sought me out and marched me in to bed. I had never in my life stayed up until midnight, although during raids I had been dragged from my sleep at all hours and taken down into the Anderson shelter, but somehow it was different to stay up all this time. I can hardly remember getting undressed and actually getting into bed, but I must have done because in the morning I was in my nightie and under the covers.

Of course, the next day, as after all good parties, there was all the clearing-up to do, and zombie-like apparitions moved slowly about the street stuffing remnants of the jollities into sacks and pushing brooms with all the zest of a spent match. I stood by the gate and watched, finding it hard to believe that these were the same people who had danced and cavorted the night before. Sheila joined me and we leant against the privet hedge, chewing stalks.

'I know what's up with that lot,' she said with a knowing nod of the head: 'they've got 'angovers, that's what.'

I didn't know what an 'angover was, but I nodded in agreement. I studied each of them carefully, but I could see nothing hanging over.

CHAPTER 15

Just three months after the jollities of VE day there were more celebrations. There was talk of something that we children were blissfully ignorant of – atom bombs – and the Japanese had surrendered, making the entire war non-existent. The jubilation that such news brought overrode any of our thoughts of questioning the grown-ups about these mysterious bombs; all we knew was that there would be more street parties, and again the street was festooned and out came the long lines of tables. The Tannoy system rattled, groaned and shrieked as we danced the night away. The bonfire was twice as big as before and someone even found some fireworks from somewhere.

Stan and Betty came home on leave, and Stan brought some brightly coloured flares, which we sent hurtling into the night sky. As soon as they had been discharged, we rushed out to join the families in the street and I got the distinct impression that the sight of an air-raid warden or a policeman would not be very welcome. Something told my childish mind, clear of any mixture of thoughts that usually bedevilled the grown-ups, that Stan had purloined these items in a nefarious manner! There was something about the whispers and the peering over shoulders while they were being lit that seemed a bit illegal! Still, they gave us great happiness while they were suspended in the night, their red and green lights bringing aahs and oohs from our lips and joy to our eyes.

Paddy was the only one of us who didn't seem to enjoy them. He didn't like the whoosh as they took off, and he stood well back and barked and barked as they finally exploded into myriads of starlets. But then he always had disliked anything in the sky, including aeroplanes, which over the last few years had been hard on him as the sky had been full of aircraft nearly every day. Spitfires were the worst – he just hated them! Well, now it seemed his days of torment were at last over because we knew that the skies would no longer be darkened, except by flocks of migrating starlings or the occasional thundercloud. Peace! What a wonderful word!

We were sad that Lila couldn't be with us for these celebrations, but she was somewhere in Scotland, and we just hoped that she was enjoying the exhilaration that we were.

A few days later there was another thing to celebrate – the street lights were going to be switched on again. I couldn't remember ever seeing them on, but at seven o'clock one evening once again the entire street was standing out the front, talking quietly and waiting. The kids sat in rows along the kerbs talking in hushed whispers. Then, all at once, they lit up. Immediately there was a great cheer and we clapped our hands and danced around in circles.

'Well, that's that!' said Dad. 'Indoors, you lot.'

And we all went inside. It seemed a bit of an anticlimax to us as we washed our hands and faces and brushed our hair ready for bed. But all good things have to come to an end, just as do bad things. The war was at last over. Done with. We had won, as we knew we would – there was never any doubt about that – but it left a sort of flat feeling. There was nothing more to look forward to – the parties were over, the street lights were on, Mum could take down those blackout curtains and school would seem empty if all the evacuees went away.

There were a few more surprises to come though, because the blackouts were transformed into skirts with coloured braid stitched round the hems. All the girls wore them. Beautiful swirly ones they were, and we twirled to make them swing. Then came yellow silk from redundant parachutes, soft as thistledown and slippery to touch. These were transformed into French knickers for the older girls and petticoats and nighties. And most of the girls in the street – or at least the older ones – were wearing silk stockings and nylons from the Americans, and we would hear funny stories of how if you walked behind a car and the exhaust blew against your legs the stockings would dissolve. I thought this very funny, although I never was able to prove whether it was right or wrong.

Eddie and Joan were very happy in each other's company and we saw more and more of him. He told us about his family in South Carolina and at times I felt that he was very homesick, but there was no talk yet of his being able to go home. He brought us lots of lovely things which were obtainable to him through what he called the PX Stores – tinned fruit, coffee, and powdered chocolate, which made a lovely drink when made with the dried milk Eddie also supplied. We were able to buy dried eggs, which made beautiful omelettes and came in little waxy boxes with an eagle on the side. Peanuts, popcorn, bottles of cherryade, sweets and chocolate bars were always on the sideboard, and Eddie made sure that the stock didn't dwindle. He brought us soft navy-blue blankets, from which we kids were given the task of removing the initials 'USMD', stitched in the corners.

From the Metal Products Reclamation Department (MPRD) we lugged home seats from aeroplanes (which made fine seats for the garden), and one day something really exciting appeared in the street. Some of the boys had disappeared for some time and at long last they turned up carrying on their heads a long metal cylinder-shaped object. We girls were immediately interested and raced down to meet them.

'What y'got there?'

'Float.'

'A what?'

'Float off a seaplane.'

'Cor!'

'What you gonna do wiv it?'

'Make a boat.'

'How're you gonna make it?'

'Cut an 'ole in it and sit in it.'

'Cor!'

In Tim Jones's dad's shed all that day, with every tool they could find, they hacked and cut and hammered, as we girls crowded round getting in the way, being cursed and sworn at, but eager to watch this wonderful craft taking shape.

'Can we 'ave a go?'

'No – boys only.'

'Rotten buggers.'

'We got it, didn't we?'

'Well, we can have a go, can't we?'

'Who's making it?'

'You are.'

'Right, then we sail in it.'

A pause – just the clang, clang of the lump hammer doing a brutal job.

''Ope it sinks.'

At long last it was ready. An oblong hole had been cut in the top, the edges turned and hammered under. It was a work of art!

'Where we gonna float it?'

They obviously hadn't thought of that because there was a long hesitation.

Mick, painting an RAF roundel on the side, his tongue sticking out in concentration, shrugged. 'Too far to carry it to the river,' he said.

'The stream's not wide enough,' grinned Margaret.

'Well, there must be somewhere,' said Johnny, looking sadly at the dry-docked flagship.

'What about White's farm? There's a pond there,' said Sheila.

So White's it was, and what a merry cavalcade marched up the road! With the craft held above our heads, one behind the other, like a silver centipede, we made our way to the farm. It was only across the main road and before long we were all heaving and shoving to get it through the hedge, because we knew that if old man White or his equally truculent sister saw us we would not be able to launch a matchbox on the pond, let alone this great cumbersome object. At last we were in the field where the pond was. It was weedy and black, but there was enough water there to take the boat, so we slipped and pulled and tugged it down the muddy sides until it was afloat. We cheered noiselessly and the boys pushed forward to be the first in, big David Robins winning. He put one long skinny leg into the hole, wavered dangerously for a second or two, then drew the other one in. Carefully he sat down. Again we cheered, silently. It turned straight over. Upside down it didn't look at all like a boat, and David came up from underneath covered in mud and weed and spluttering.

We were awestruck. No one had thought that it wouldn't float. It was a dreadful shock.

'Soddin' thing,' said David as he squelched up the bank to where we stood open-mouthed and silent.

'Silly damned thing, anyway,' said Mick, and off they went, leaving Margaret, Sheila, Joy, Annie and me staring in disbelief. We had hoped that after a good sail round on the pond the boys might relent and let us have a go. Now they had gone.

Annie reached out and pulled the wallowing metal tube to the side.

'Gissa 'and,' she said, and, unquestioningly, we did as she bid.

An hour later we had wedged the thing between the banks of our stream and were sitting in it, pretending we were Betty Grable and Don Ameche canoeing in the moonlight. It made a superb 'pretend' boat. It couldn't tip over because there was no room, and with about four inches of water underneath there was certainly no danger of the soaking that David had got!

The confidence that VJ day brought showed in numerous ways. Dad began to hang his strings of onions in the Anderson shelter and allowed us to play there quite openly. Gran and Grampy decided that they wanted to go home, and we saw them off with all their bag and baggage piled in a removal van. I cried because Grampy had gone – I really loved that old man – but I felt that things would be a little easier for me now that Gran with all her stern ways had departed. She wasn't a bad old soul, I supposed, graciously, but the sight of that van bearing her away lifted my spirits.

More and more children suddenly found that they had dads again and, each time one of them was due home, up would go the banners outside the relevant houses – usually a bed sheet rashly sacrificed and written on with lipstick or paint saying things like 'Well done, Bill' and 'Welcome home, Dad'. All day the Union Jacks would fly until at last the returning hero would appear and be hugged and kissed and cuddled all the way to his front door.

The Italian prisoners were allowed more freedom, and it was

quite normal to see them in the pictures, no longer in their dull green but in rust-coloured uniforms with yellow patches on them. They were a friendly lot and we would chat to them whenever we met them in the street.

'Them Eyeties are OK,' said John one evening as we sat at each end of the table doing our homework.

I, as usual, had twice as much to do because we had an agreement (his idea) that French and English would always be done by me and maths was his. I frowned over the books spread in disarray over the cloth.

'Why?' I asked.

'Well, they bother to talk to us, don't they?' He opened my geometry case. 'Can I borrow this?' He held up a set square.

I nodded. 'We don't see Germans on the street,' I said. 'They might talk to us if they were allowed out.'

'We couldn't understand them if they did,' he answered.

I scanned the page before me in a desperate attempt to find the French for 'The train was late', and wondered if German would be any easier to learn.

'The Italians don't speak proper English either, but they try.'

Mum came into the room with a basket of ironing.

'Are you two going to be much longer? I need the table for ironing.'

Her old home-made board had long ago given up the ghost. Mum looked desperately tired, no doubt from hours and hours of work. We scuffled the books in to one corner and moved our chairs closer together to give her room, and she spread a folded blanket on the table. She glanced at the clock on the mantelpiece.

'Dad's very late,' she said.

'Where is he?' I asked.

'He went up the allotment ages ago to get some spuds and a marrow, but he said he wouldn't be long. I wonder what's happened.'

She ironed in silence for a while, but she kept looking up at the clock. John kicked me gently under the table and nodded his head in her direction. I nodded. I understood what he meant.

'Shall we go and look for him?' I asked. It was beginning to get dark.

'Yes, I think so, but stay together.'

We promised her that we would, and went off, shrugging into our coats as we did so.

There was the usual gang standing on the corner and they called out to us, anxious to know where we were off to, hoping that we had come up with a brilliant idea of how to pass the evening. When we explained, they were all eager to help and we decided that now there were quite a few of us we could split up into groups. This way we could cover all the paths to and from the allotments and so not miss him if he was on his way home.

Annie, Johnny Winters and I took the road down the Slade and round past Wingfield Hospital into Old Road. This took us to the same lane where we had nearly been caught scrumping and John had been trapped in the tree. That seemed years ago. By the time we reached the five-barred gate it was quite dark and the avenue of trees looked forbidding. We hesitated by the gate and stared in apprehension into the darkness.

'He wouldn't come this way, would he? He'd go across by the Horses' Field. It's quicker.'

Johnny was hopeful: 'The others have gone that way – they'll find him.'

'I didn't ask Mum if he had the wheelbarrow,' I said, peering into the gloom. 'If he did he'd come this way, because of the rough ground the other way.'

Annie, her arms holding her coat round her because of the cold night air, shivered. 'It's bloody dark down there,' she said.

'But we should go and look,' I said.

'Perhaps if we wait here a while he'll come along anyway.'

Johnny was not so bold without the rest of the gang. He leant over the gate, trying to see if there was any sign of Dad, with or without his wheelbarrow.

After a while Annie said, 'There's something under the hedge over there,' and pointed into the lane.

Johnny and I stood up on the bottom rail of the gate and followed her finger.

'Where?' I asked.

'Over there.'

'Oh, yeah, so there is,' said Johnny.

There was indeed something lying there, and, of course, the more we tried to distinguish what it was the more it took the shape of a body.

'Perhaps he's fallen down and broken his leg,' said Annie. 'If he has he's probably been lying there for ages.'

By now my imaginative mind could see quite clearly that the shape was indeed Dad. I could feel the hair standing up on the back of my neck and my legs began to shake uncontrollably.

'Oh, God,' I whispered.

'Let's get help,' said Johnny, turning to go.

'No!' I almost shouted, and began to climb the gate.

Annie dragged at my coat. 'You can't go over there,' she said.

'I can – it's my dad. He's hurt.'

Voices sounded in the darkness and the gang appeared through the black depths of the lane. Someone was flashing a torch. It was Tim Jones.

'Over there!' I yelled. 'Under them bushes!'

He shone the torch where I pointed. He peered, head lowered, and moved forward slowly, the torch like a yellow lance before him. We all waited with bated breath. Then he put out a foot and gingerly probed at the 'thing'.

'Cement bags,' he said. 'That's what they are – cement bags.'

The relief that it wasn't Dad overwhelmed me, and first I giggled then the tears came. Everyone seemed to be chattering at once. They had been up through the Horses' Field and along the little stony track that led to the allotments past Piggy Lee's sties, first to our allotment and then on to Grampy Hathaway's, but there had been no sign of Dad.

My howls grew louder. 'Where can he be?' I wailed.

Annie put her arms round me. 'He'll be all right,' she soothed.

'Yeah, 'course he will,' they all agreed.

'Can we help?' – a man's voice from behind us.

We turned and looked aghast at the two German POWs standing there.

'Bloody 'ell – Germans,' said someone, and once again, as we always did when something scared us, we fled. In one long helter-skelter rush we made it to the familiarity of the street. Huffing and puffing, we clustered together by the flats.

'What d'you think they were doing there?'

'They'd escaped, that's what.'

'Blimey! Shouldn't we report it or something?'

'Yeah, we should. There might be thousands of 'em wandering about.'

A pause.

'Go on, then,' said Annie.

'Go on what?' Johnny said, pushing his hands deep into his pockets and hunching his shoulders.

'Report 'em.'

'Why me?' he asked.

'You're the oldest.' It seemed as good a reason as any.

'No, I'm not.' He looked round wildly, then pointed to Tim. 'He is.'

Then there ensued a terrific argument – birthdates were bandied about and there was a great deal of rushing and shoving.

Annie watched, turned to me and said, 'Oh, sod the Germans – I'm going in.'

'What about my dad?' I asked.

She shrugged her shoulders. 'Perhaps he's home already.'

And indeed he was. When I got indoors he was washing his hands in the kitchen sink, his muddy wellingtons already discarded and a pile of vegetables stacked on the draining board. I was so relieved to see him that I put my arms round his waist and laid my head against his back. The tears were stabbing at my eyes.

'I shall have to stay out late chattering again!' he smiled.

He had been chatting to one of his gardening friends in one of the sheds, no doubt sharing a glass of beer, and neither of them had noticed that it had got so late. I was so elated that I quite forgot about the 'escaped' prisoners until John came in later.

'We saw some Germans tonight – out of their camp, they were. Just walking about, weren't they, Nan?' he said.

Mum looked aghast. 'In the street?' she asked.

'Yes, they spoke to us,' I said, struggling to untie my laces. How did a perfectly normal bow get itself into such a tangle?

'Spoke to you?' Mum took my foot in her hands and picked at the knots. 'What do you mean?'

'They wanted to help us look for Dad, I think,' I said.

'Oh, lor!' She loosened my shoe and slipped it off, taking up the other one. 'Ted, did you hear this?'

Dad listened to our story, frowned as he lit his roll-up, and said that we must never talk to them or show friendship in any way. 'I don't know what they are thinking about, letting prisoners walk about all over the place,' he said.

He threw the spent match into the fire.

'The Eyeties do,' I said. 'They go to the pictures an' all.'

'They're different,' said Dad.

'How?' asked John.

Dad thought for a moment or two, puffing smoke from pursed lips.

'Well, they just are,' he said.

'Annie said they'd escaped,' I said.

'Oh, lor,' said Mum again.

With that we were sent to bed and I lay awake thinking about those cement bags under the hedge. They certainly had looked like a body lying there. And I thought, too, about the two Germans. Perhaps they really had just wanted to help. What must they have thought of us, running away like that! I said my prayers and asked God to make sure that when they were recaptured their guards wouldn't be too harsh with them.

CHAPTER 16

Sheila's sister Kathleen had married Bert Tanner, and, much to my dismay, her wedding was as pretty as Betty's had been. He was a perky little Cockney, small-boned like his mother, and he always made Sheila and me laugh with his jokes and funny expressions. When he came home on leave we would sit on their back step and roar with laughter, then Kathleen, who was a reserved sort of girl, would reprimand him gently and we would lose him.

'Nice, ain't he?' Sheila would say, and I had to agree. All the Tanners were lovely people and I was as pleased as Sheila that they were not going back to London, but wanted to stay in Oxford forever.

Annie's family, too, were staying. We sat in the long grass in the dell one afternoon watching an ants' nest with great interest, and she just said, 'We're staying 'ere!'

I gave the nest another prod with a grass stalk to get the activity going again.

'Staying where?' I asked.

''Ere, in Oxford,' she answered.

'Not going back to London?'

'No – my mum says that she don't want to and my dad says that he don't want to neither, so we're staying.' She wiped a couple of ants from her leg. 'What d'you fink?'

What did I think? What a silly thing to ask! Auntie Dolly had gone, Cousin Sheila had gone, Barda had gone, Gran and Grampy had gone! But Annie was staying!

'Let's go and catch newts,' I said happily.

We hadn't had much luck with our 'newting' when across from the direction of the golf links, leaping our stream and sploshing through the oozing black mud, came fifteen or so men in shorts and singlets. They puffed and panted up the little bank to where we stood watching, past us and on up through the dell, a long, sweating muddy line of flailing arms and legs. We could hear them calling to each other regarding the correct way to go and realised that they were German.

'God!' said Annie. 'Fancy letting them run about all over the place like that.'

I agreed that it seemed a strange thing to do – to let prisoners run loose, and when we got home again we told Mum about it.

Joan, her hair wrapped in a towel, her face rosy from bathing, said that in Headington they were walking about like anybody else, in and out of shops and even queueing up at the pictures. She unwound the towel and propped her little tin of Dinkie curlers on the mantelpiece in front of the mirror. 'After all,' she said, combing out a strand of wet hair, 'the war is over.'

'It may be over,' said Mum, 'but you have just reminded me that the new ration books have got to be collected from Old Headington on Monday. There's a list on the wall in the Co-op, and it's sort of broken down into groups. If your name starts with anything between A and G they can be collected today, Saturday, but as ours begins with H we've got to get ours on Monday. The place is open till nine o'clock at night, so I thought that when you get home from work you could do it for me.'

Joan frowned. 'I don't think Eddie's coming round.'

'Even if he is,' said Mum, 'those books have got to be picked up.'

'I'll come with you, Joan,' I offered.

'And me,' said Annie, who was standing by the open back door.

So on Monday after tea Joan, Annie and I set off for Old Headington. What a sight met our eyes! The queue was almost the length of the High Street. Joan stopped dead in her tracks.

'Crikey,' she said. 'We'll be here all night.'

We joined the end of the winding, chattering, glum-faced line clutching the tatty bundle of used ration books, Annie doing cat's cradle with a loop of red wool. Her fingers worked deftly, and at intervals she would hold it out for us to see.

'A lamp post,' she would say, or 'An aeroplane.'

Joan took it from her and twined her fingers round it, twisting this way and that and finally turning the whole thing inside out.

'Cup and saucer,' she said.

The next twenty minutes or so were taken up in teaching us how to do this wonderful trick, and as we worked away the man in front of us was overheard to say to the lady with him, 'Did you bring our identity cards, Mabel?'

She reached into her capacious shopping bag and held them aloft. He nodded and smiled. Joan looked at me and I looked at her. We hadn't been told to bring *them*.

'You'd better run home and get them, Nan,' said Joan in a whisper.

It was some way to go and I hesitated.

'Coming, Annie?'

She leant against the high stone wall of someone's garden and frowned at the wool. Her face told me that she didn't fancy that long run home.

I looked at the column stretching into eternity before us. There would be plenty of time. I set off at a run, not stopping for a breather until I reached the roundabout at Old Road. There was a wooden seat under the big chestnut tree and I fell gratefully on to it. My legs, still wanting to run, rested while I regained my spent breath. Then I set off again on the last leg of the journey. Mum was bathing Pat when I reached home.

'That was quick,' she smiled. 'I didn't expect you back for ages.'

'We're not.'

I explained about the identity cards and she rummaged in the dresser drawer. I took them and started back. Out of breath and aching from my knees downwards, I finally made it. To my astonishment Joan and Annie hardly seemed to have moved.

The ladies giving out the new books were seated at long trestle tables piled high with books – green, blue and off-white. A fat lady in a blue twinset, her jacket hung carelessly round her shoulders, beckoned us forward as we finally reached them. She took our cards, wrote things on her big sheet of paper and handed Joan the books. Then she wrote again, something from our identity cards, and handed them back, too. It was quite dark by this time, and we hurried home glad to have completed the job.

'Good job we heard that man saying about the cards, wasn't it?' I said.

Joan nodded. She was very quiet all the way home and I wondered what had upset her. Annie kept up a constant chatter, ran along walls and picked pieces from people's hedges.

When we got indoors, having deposited Annie at her house, Joan turned on me angrily.

'Don't you ever bring that girl anywhere with me again,' she said. 'She's disgusting.'

I couldn't think what Annie could have done that was so awful, so I asked why.

'She shamed me in that queue, that's what she did. First of all she called a lady a nosy old cow because she asked how long we'd been waiting and where we were from. Then she brought out the most disgusting bit of rag to wipe her nose. Honestly, it was filthy. Then guess what she did. She stood there picking her nose!' Joan threw her coat over the back of the armchair in disgust.

Annie always did pick her nose. She never used a hanky, always just a piece of sheeting or something, and she did have the habit of cleaning her inkwell at school with it, and sometimes wiped the mud off her shoes with it if we'd been down the dell before school. These were just things that I had accepted as Annie, so they neither shocked nor disgusted me. I hadn't thought that other people might not like them. As for the 'nosy old cow' bit – well, that again was Annie. I accepted her from the day I first saw her under the bushes as she was, warts and all. These silly things didn't matter at all. She was my friend.

'You're a snob, our Joan,' I said.

'No, I'm not – but you must admit she's a bit awful, isn't she?'

'No, she's not! I was on the defensive for my friend and felt my cheeks begin to burn.

'She shamed me amongst all those people. Some of those people are customers in our shop. They know me!' She bent her head to undo her shoes.

I didn't like to think of my Joan being shamed, but I had started to champion Annie so I had to continue. 'Well, I'm very sorry about that,' I said sarcastically, 'but Annie's all right.'

'Well, I just hope that you don't pick up any of her filthy habits, that's all,' said Joan, and she swept out of the room.

From that day, whether I had started to grow up or not, I began to watch people's habits – the hair-twirlers, the nail-biters, the thumb-suckers and, of course, the nose-pickers. I hadn't realised until now that Annie spent most of her waking hours with her finger up her nose. I also had missed the fact that Sheila twirled her hair and sucked the ends, that Joy nibbled constantly at her nails and fingers and that Shirley Bye sucked her thumb. I asked Mum why they did it, and she said that most of it was because of nerves and that as a baby I had sucked my right index finger almost to a point! I was appalled! Nevertheless I began to feel differently towards Annie, although I tried very hard to blot out certain things. I began to notice the holes in her socks, and the trodden-down heels of her shoes, the drooping hem of her skirt and the buttons that were not where they should be on her coat. Safety pins do not look nice on a coat, and I told her so and received a stinging slap across the face for my pains.

'Mind your own soddin' business,' she spat at me.

'Well, I'm only telling you because it makes you look scruffy, that's all.'

I rubbed my cheek hard and tried not to let the tears come.

'So what!' she hissed. 'What's it to you? You've just got all stuck-up since you've been at that Central.'

I tried to pull my gabardine raincoat tighter round me to hide the navy gymslip and green girdle, the crisp white blouse and the green-and-navy tie. For the first time since I put it on I was almost ashamed of it.

'No, I haven't,' I protested.

But somewhere inside I knew that I was changing. Central was so different from Margaret Road Junior. Most of the girls came from roads with bay-windowed semis and their fathers had cars. I had invited some of them to play, but they were obviously not comfortable sloshing through the swampy bits or groping about in the stream. Climbing the big willow was not what they liked to do, and they found it almost impossible to clamber up on to the air-raid shelters. My beloved old Anderson shelter caused them to wrinkle their noses at the musty smell, so my home life and school life were segregated, totally.

I sat one day in the gloomy interior of the Anderson shelter and decided that I had to be two completely separate people. In school uniform I was Anne, straight-backed and tidy, that navy velour hat held firmly in place by elastic under the chin. I spoke nicely and never ran – ladies do not run even if their bus home is about to leave. My socks were not allowed to wrinkle at the ankles and I said 'please' and 'thank you'. At playtimes I sat quietly on a bench; I didn't play chase or anything unladylike. I would have loved to play 'all in together' with a skipping rope, climb the school walls to see what was on the other side, and run, run. . . .

I looked up into the rusting corrugation of the roof and realised that my wonderful carefree days of window-breaker tops, slugs in jars, soggy socks, bright glassy marbles, and even the bitter little arguments with friends were slipping away from me. My eyes could make out the strings of onions Dad had hung in the corner and the box of apples from Grampy Hathaway's tree on the allotment on one end of the bench. It seemed such a long time ago when all the aunties, uncles, cousins, Mum and Dad and all the family, Paddy curled up on Grampy's lap, had sung Christmas carols in here. I had stuck pictures of Randolph Scott and Gary Cooper on the back of the door, but the old Anderson shelter was still the same to me. I hoped Dad would keep it here for ever and ever, but he had already mentioned that if it were dug up it would make a good bike shed.

Nothing changes, they say, but it does. Everything changes. Most of all, people.

I took one last look round, screwed up the letter I had been writing to Barda – and went indoors.